# Harvard
# Business
# Review

ON

MANAGING

UNCERTAINTY

# THE HARVARD BUSINESS REVIEW PAPERBACK SERIES

The series is designed to bring today's managers and professionals the fundamental information they need to stay competitive in a fast-moving world. From the preeminent thinkers whose work has defined an entire field to the rising stars who will redefine the way we think about business, here are the leading minds and landmark ideas that have established the *Harvard Business Review* as required reading for ambitious businesspeople in organizations around the globe.

Other books in the series:

*Harvard Business Review on the Business Value of IT*

*Harvard Business Review on Change*

*Harvard Business Review on Entrepreneurship*

*Harvard Business Review on Knowledge Management*

*Harvard Business Review on Leadership*

*Harvard Business Review on Managing People*

*Harvard Business Review on Measuring Corporate Performance*

*Harvard Business Review on Nonprofits*

*Harvard Business Review on Strategies for Growth*

# Harvard Business Review

## ON

### MANAGING

### UNCERTAINTY

A HARVARD BUSINESS REVIEW PAPERBACK

The *Harvard Business Review* articles in this collection are available as individual reprints. Discounts apply to quantity pur-
chases. For information and ordering, please contact Customer
Service, Harvard Business School Publishing, Boston, MA 02163.
Telephone: (617) 496-1449, 8 A.M. to 6 P.M. Eastern Time, Monday through Friday. Fax: (617) 496-1029, 24 hours a day. E-mail:
custserv@hbsp.harvard.edu

**Library of Congress Cataloging-in-Publication Data**
Harvard business review on managing uncertainty.
         p.   cm.—(Harvard business review paperback series)
     A collection of articles previously published in the Harvard
business review.
     Includes bibliographical references and index.
     ISBN 0-87584-908-3
     1. Strategic planning.   2. Uncertainty.   I. Harvard business
review.   II. Title: Managing uncertainty.   III. Series.
HD30.28.H379   1999
658.4'012—dc21                                                    98-31397
                                                                        CIP

*The paper used in this publication meets the requirements of the
American National Standard for Permanence of Paper for Printed
Library Materials Z39.49-1984.*

# Contents

# Strategy Under Uncertainty

HUGH COURTNEY,

JANE KIRKLAND, AND

PATRICK VIGUERIE

## Executive Summary

AT THE HEART OF THE TRADITIONAL APPROACH to strategy lies the assumption that by applying a set of powerful analytic tools, executives can predict the future of any
business accurately enough to allow them to choose a
clear strategic direction. But what happens when the
environment is so uncertain that no amount of analysis
will allow us to predict the future? What makes for a
good strategy in highly uncertain business environments?

The authors, consultants at McKinsey & Company,
argue that uncertainty requires a new way of thinking
about strategy. All too often, they say, executives take a
binary view: either they underestimate uncertainty to
come up with the forecasts required by their companies'
planning or capital-budgeting processes, or they overesti-
mate it, abandon all analysis, and go with their gut
instinct.

1

The authors outline a new approach that begins by making a crucial distinction among four discrete levels of uncertainty that any company might face. They then explain how a set of generic strategies—shaping the market, adapting to it, or reserving the right to play at a later time—can be used in each of the four levels. And they illustrate how these strategies can be implemented through a combination of three basic types of actions: big bets, options, and no-regrets moves.

The framework can help managers determine which analytic tools can inform decision making under uncertainty—and which cannot. At a broader level, it offers executives a discipline for thinking rigorously and systematically about uncertainty and its implications for strategy.

---

WHAT MAKES FOR A GOOD STRATEGY in highly uncertain business environments? Some executives seek to shape the future with high-stakes bets. Eastman Kodak Company, for example, is spending $500 million per year to develop an array of digital photography products that it hopes will fundamentally change the way people create, store, and view pictures. Meanwhile, Hewlett-Packard Company is investing $50 million per year to pursue a rival vision centered around home-based photo printers. The business press loves to hype such industry-shaping strategies because of their potential to create enormous wealth, but the sober reality is that most companies lack the industry position, assets, or appetite for risk necessary to make such strategies work.

More risk-averse executives hedge their bets by making a number of smaller investments. In pursuit of growth opportunities in emerging markets, for example, many consumer-product companies are forging limited operational or distribution alliances. But it's often difficult to determine if such limited investments truly reserve the right to play in these countries or just reserve the right to lose.

Alternatively, some executives favor investments in flexibility that allow their companies to adapt quickly as markets evolve. But the costs of establishing such flexibility can be high. Moreover, taking a wait-and-see strategy—postponing large investments until the future becomes clear—can create a window of opportunity for competitors.

*Under uncertainty, traditional approaches to strategic planning can be downright dangerous.*

How should executives facing great uncertainty decide whether to bet big, hedge, or wait and see? Chances are, traditional strategic-planning processes won't help much. The standard practice is to lay out a vision of future events precise enough to be captured in a discounted-cash-flow analysis. Of course, managers can discuss alternative scenarios and test how sensitive their forecasts are to changes in key variables, but the goal of such analysis is often to find the most likely outcome and create a strategy based on it. That approach serves companies well in relatively stable business environments. But when there is greater uncertainty about the future, it is at best marginally helpful and at worst downright dangerous.

One danger is that this traditional approach leads executives to view uncertainty in a binary way—to assume that the world is either certain, and therefore open to precise predictions about the future, or uncertain, and therefore completely unpredictable. Planning

or capital-budgeting processes that require point forecasts force managers to bury underlying uncertainties in
their cash flows. Such systems clearly push managers to
underestimate uncertainty in order to make a compelling case for their strategy.

Underestimating uncertainty can lead to strategies
that neither defend against the threats nor take advantage of the opportunities that higher levels of uncertainty may provide. In one of the most colossal underes-
timations in business history, Kenneth H. Olsen, then
president of Digital Equipment Corporation, announced
in 1977 that "there is no reason for any individual to
have a computer in their home." The explosion in the
personal computer market was not inevitable in 1977,
but it was certainly within the range of possibilities that
industry experts were discussing at the time.

At the other extreme, assuming that the world is
entirely unpredictable can lead managers to abandon
the analytical rigor of their traditional planning processes altogether and base their strategic decisions primarily on gut instinct. This "just do it" approach to
strategy can cause executives to place misinformed
bets on emerging products or markets that result in
record write-offs. Those who took the plunge and invested in home banking in the early 1980s immediately
come to mind.

Risk-averse managers who think they are in very
uncertain environments don't trust their gut instincts
and suffer from decision paralysis. They avoid making
critical strategic decisions about the products, markets,
and technologies they should develop. They focus
instead on reengineering, quality management, or internal cost-reduction programs. Although valuable, those
programs are not substitutes for strategy.

Making systematically sound strategic decisions
under uncertainty requires a different approach—one
that avoids this dangerous binary view. It is rare that
managers know absolutely nothing of strategic importance, even in the most uncertain environments. In fact,
they usually can identify a range of potential outcomes
or even a discrete set of scenarios. This simple insight is
extremely powerful because determining which strategy
is best, and what process should be used to develop it,
depend vitally on the level of uncertainty a company
faces.

What follows, then, is a framework for determining
the level of uncertainty surrounding strategic decisions
and for tailoring strategy to that uncertainty. No
approach can make the challenges of uncertainty go
away, but this one offers practical guidance that will
lead to more informed and confident strategic decisions.

## Four Levels of Uncertainty

Even the most uncertain business environments contain
a lot of strategically relevant information. First, it is
often possible to identify clear trends, such as market
demographics, that can help define potential demand
for future products or services. Second, there is usually a
host of factors that are currently *unknown* but that are
in fact *knowable*—that could be known if the right analysis were done. Performance attributes for current technologies, elasticities of demand for certain stable categories of products, and competitors' capacity-expansion
plans are variables that are often unknown, but not
entirely unknowable.

The uncertainty that remains after the best possible analysis has been done is what we call *residual*

*uncertainty*—for example, the outcome of an ongoing regulatory debate or the performance attributes of a technology still in development. But often, quite a bit can be known about even those residual uncertainties. (See figure "How to Use the Four Levels of Uncertainty.") In practice, we have found that the residual uncertainty facing most strategic-decision makers falls into one of four broad levels:

## LEVEL 1: CLEAR-ENOUGH FUTURE

At level 1, managers can develop a single forecast of the future that is precise *enough* for strategy development. Although it will be inexact to the degree that all business environments are inherently uncertain, the forecast will be sufficiently narrow to point to a single strategic

---

### How to Use the Four Levels of Uncertainty

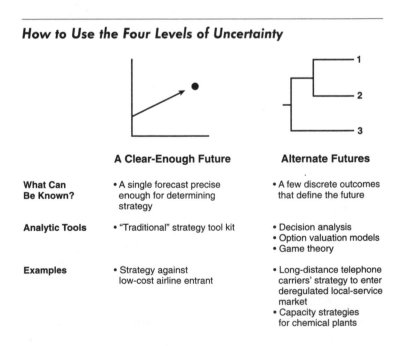

|  | A Clear-Enough Future | Alternate Futures |
|---|---|---|
| **What Can Be Known?** | • A single forecast precise enough for determining strategy | • A few discrete outcomes that define the future |
| **Analytic Tools** | • "Traditional" strategy tool kit | • Decision analysis<br>• Option valuation models<br>• Game theory |
| **Examples** | • Strategy against low-cost airline entrant | • Long-distance telephone carriers' strategy to enter deregulated local-service market<br>• Capacity strategies for chemical plants |

direction. In other words, at level 1, the residual uncertainty is irrelevant to making strategic decisions.

Consider a major airline trying to develop a strategic response to the entry of a low-cost, no-frills competitor into one of its hub airports. Should it respond with a low-cost service of its own? Should it cede the low-cost niche segments to the new entrant? Or should it compete aggressively on price and service in an attempt to drive the entrant out of the market?

To make that strategic decision, the airline's executives need market research on the size of different customer segments and the likely response of each segment to different combinations of pricing and service. They also need to know how much it costs the competitor to serve, and how much capacity the competitor has for, every route in question. Finally, the executives need to

---

| **A Range of Futures** | **True Ambiguity** |
|---|---|
| • A range of possible outcomes, but no natural scenarios | • No basis to forecast the future |
| • Latent-demand research<br>• Technology forecasting<br>• Scenario planning | • Analogies and pattern recognition<br>• Nonlinear dynamic models |
| • Entering emerging markets, such as India<br>• Developing or acquiring emerging technologies in consumer electronics | • Entering the market for consumer multimedia applications<br>• Entering the Russian market in 1992 |

know the new entrant's competitive objectives to anticipate how it would respond to any strategic moves their
airline might make. In today's U.S. airline industry, such
information is either known already or is possible to
know. It might not be easy to obtain—it might require
new market research, for example—but it is inherently
knowable. And once that information is known, residual
uncertainty would be limited, and the incumbent airline
would be able to build a confident business case around
its strategy.

## LEVEL 2: ALTERNATE FUTURES

At level 2, the future can be described as one of a few
alternate outcomes, or *discrete scenarios*. Analysis
cannot identify which outcome will occur, although it
may help establish probabilities. Most important, some,
if not all, elements of the strategy would change if the
outcome were predictable.

Many businesses facing major regulatory or legislative change confront level 2 uncertainty. Consider U.S.
long-distance telephone providers in late 1995, as they
began developing strategies for entering local telephone
markets. By late 1995, legislation that would fundamentally deregulate the industry was pending in Congress,
and the broad form that new regulations would take was
fairly clear to most industry observers. But whether or
not the legislation was going to pass and how quickly it
would be implemented in the event it did pass were
uncertain. No amount of analysis would allow the long-
distance carriers to predict those outcomes, and the correct course of action—for example, the timing of investments in network infrastructure—depended on which
outcome occurred.

In another common level 2 situation, the value of a strategy depends mainly on competitors' strategies, and those cannot yet be observed or predicted. For example, in oligopoly markets, such as those for pulp and paper, chemicals, and basic raw materials, the primary uncertainty is often competitors' plans for expanding capacity: Will they build new plants or not? Economies of scale often dictate that any plant built would be quite large and would be likely to have a significant impact on industry prices and profitability. Therefore, any one company's decision to build a plant is often contingent on competitors' decisions. This is a classic level 2 situation: The possible outcomes are discrete and clear. It is difficult to predict which one will occur. And the best strategy depends on which one does occur.

## LEVEL 3: A RANGE OF FUTURES

At level 3, a range of potential futures can be identified. That range is defined by a limited number of key variables, but the actual outcome may lie anywhere along a continuum bounded by that range. There are no natural discrete scenarios. As in level 2, some, and possibly all, elements of the strategy would change if the outcome were predictable.

Companies in emerging industries or entering new geographic markets often face level 3 uncertainty. Consider a European consumer-goods company deciding whether to introduce its products to the Indian market. The best possible market research might identify only a broad range of potential customer-penetration rates—say, from 10% to 30%—and there would be no obvious scenarios within that range. Such a broad

range of estimates would be common when introducing completely new products and services to a market, and therefore determining the level of latent
demand is very difficult. The company entering India
would be likely to follow a very different and more
aggressive entry strategy if it knew for certain that its
customer penetration rates would be closer to 30%
than to 10%.

Analogous problems exist for companies in fields
driven by technological innovation, such as the semi-
conductor industry. When deciding whether to invest
in a new technology, producers can often estimate
only a broad range of potential cost and performance
attributes for the technology, and the overall profitability of the investment depends on those attributes.

### LEVEL 4: TRUE AMBIGUITY

At level 4, multiple dimensions of uncertainty interact to
create an environment that is virtually impossible to
predict. Unlike in level 3 situations, the range of potential outcomes cannot be identified, let alone scenarios
within that range. It might not even be possible to identify, much less predict, all the relevant variables that will
define the future.

Level 4 situations are quite rare, and they tend to
migrate toward one of the other levels over time. Nevertheless, they do exist. Consider a telecommunications
company deciding where and how to compete in the
emerging consumer-multimedia market. It is confronting multiple uncertainties concerning technology,
demand, and relationships between hardware and content providers, all of which may interact in ways so
unpredictable that no plausible range of scenarios can
be identified.

Companies considering making major entry investments in post-Communist Russia in 1992 faced level 4
uncertainty. They could not outline the potential laws or
regulations that would govern property rights and transactions. That central uncertainty was compounded by
additional uncertainty over the viability of supply chains
and the demand for previously unavailable consumer
goods and services. And shocks such as a political assas-
sination or a currency default could have spun the whole
system toward completely unforeseen outcomes.

Those examples illustrate how difficult strategic decisions can be at level 4, but they also underscore their
transitory nature. Greater political and regulatory stability has turned decisions about whether to enter Russian
markets into level 3 problems for the majority of industries today. Similarly, uncertainty about strategic decisions in the consumer multimedia market will migrate
to level 3 or to level 2 as the industry begins to take
shape over the next several years.

## Tailoring Strategic Analysis to the Four Levels of Uncertainty

Our experience suggests that at least half of all strategy
problems fall into levels 2 or 3, while most of the rest are
level 1 problems. But executives who think about uncertainty in a binary way tend to treat all strategy problems
as if they fell into either level 1 or level 4. And when
those executives base their strategies on rigorous analysis, they are most likely to apply the same set of analytic
tools regardless of the level of residual uncertainty they
face. For example, they might attempt to use standard,
quantitative market-research techniques to forecast
demand for data traffic over wireless communications
networks as far out as ten years from now.

But, in fact, a different kind of analysis should be done to identify and evaluate strategy options at each level of uncertainty. All strategy making begins with some form of situation analysis—that is, a picture of what the world will look like today and what is likely to happen in the future. Identifying the levels of uncertainty thus helps define the best such an analysis can do to describe each possible future an industry faces.

To help generate level 1's usefully precise prediction of the future, managers can use the standard strategy tool kit—market research, analyses of competitors' costs and capacity, value chain analysis, Michael Porter's five-forces framework, and so on. A discounted-cash-flow model that incorporates those predictions can then be used to determine the value of various alternative strategies. It's not surprising that most managers feel extremely comfortable in level 1 situations—these are the tools and frameworks taught in every leading business program in the United States.

Level 2 situations are a bit more complex. First, managers must develop a set of discrete scenarios based on their understanding of how the key residual uncertainties might play out—for example, whether deregulation occurs or not, a competitor builds a new plant or not. Each scenario may require a different valuation model—general industry structure and conduct will often be fundamentally different depending on which scenario occurs, so alternative valuations can't be handled by performing sensitivity analyses around a single baseline model. Getting information that helps establish the relative probabilities of the alternative outcomes should be a high priority.

After establishing an appropriate valuation model for each possible outcome and determining how probable each is likely to be, a classic decision-analysis framework can be used to evaluate the risks and returns inherent in alternative strategies. This process will identify the likely winners and losers in alternative scenarios, and perhaps more important, it will help quantify what's at stake for companies that follow status quo strategies. Such an analysis is often the key to making the case for strategic change.

In level 2 situations, it is important not only to identify the different possible future outcomes but also to think through the likely paths the industry might take to reach those alternative futures. Will change occur in major steps at some particular point in time, following, for example, a regulatory ruling or a competitor's decision to enter the market? Or will change occur in a more evolutionary fashion, as often happens after a resolution of competing technology standards? This is vital information because it determines which market signals or trigger variables should be monitored closely. As events unfold and the relative probabilities of alternative scenarios change, it is likely that one's strategy will also need to be adapted to these changes.

At one level, the analysis in level 3 is very similar to that in level 2. A set of scenarios needs to be identified that describes alternative future outcomes, and analysis should focus on the trigger events signaling that the market is moving toward one or another scenario. Developing a meaningful set of scenarios, however, is less straightforward in level 3. Scenarios that describe the extreme points in the range of possible outcomes are often relatively easy to develop, but these rarely provide much concrete guidance for current strategic decisions. Since there are no other natural discrete scenarios in level 3, deciding which possible outcomes should be fully developed into alternative scenarios is a real art. But there are a few general rules. First, develop only a limited number of alternative scenarios—the complexity of juggling more than four or five tends to hinder decision making. Second, avoid developing redundant scenarios that have no unique implications for strategic decision making; make sure each scenario offers a distinct picture of the industry's structure, conduct, and performance. Third, develop a set of scenarios that collectively account for the *probable* range of future outcomes and not necessarily the entire *possible* range.

Because it is impossible in level 3 to define a complete list of scenarios and related probabilities, it is impossible to calculate the expected value of different strategies. However, establishing the range of scenarios should allow managers to determine how robust their strategy is, identify likely winners and losers, and determine roughly the risk of following status quo strategies.

*At level 4, it is critical to avoid the urge to throw up your hands and act purely on gut instinct.*

Situation analysis at level 4 is even more qualitative. Still, it is critical to avoid the urge to throw one's hands up and act purely on gut instinct. Instead, managers need to catalog systematically what they know and what is possible to know. Even if it is impossible to develop a meaningful set of probable, or even possible, outcomes in level 4 situations, managers can gain valuable strategic perspective. Usually, they can identify at least a subset of the variables that will determine how the market will evolve over time—for example, customer penetration rates or technology performance attributes. And they can identify favorable and unfavorable indicators of these variables that will let them track the market's evolution over time and adapt their strategy as new information becomes available.

Managers can also identify patterns indicating possible ways the market may evolve by studying how analogous markets developed in other level 4 situations, determining the key attributes of the winners and losers in those situations and identifying the strategies they employed. Finally, although it will be impossible to quantify the risks and returns of different strategies, managers should be able

*The old one-size-fits-all analytic approach to evaluating strategy options is simply inadequate.*

to identify what information they would have to believe about the future to justify the investments they are considering. Early market indicators and analogies from similar markets will help sort out whether such beliefs are realistic or not.

Uncertainty demands a more flexible approach to situation analysis. The old one-size-fits-all approach is simply inadequate. Over time, companies in most industries will face strategy problems that have varying levels of residual uncertainty, and it is vitally important that the strategic analysis be tailored to the level of uncertainty.

## Postures and Moves

Before we can talk about the dynamics of formulating strategy at each level of uncertainty, we need to introduce a basic vocabulary for talking about strategy. First, there are three *strategic postures* a company can choose to take vis-à-vis uncertainty: shaping, adapting, or reserving the right to play. Second, there are three types of moves in *the portfolio of actions* that can be used to implement that strategy: big bets, options, and no-regrets moves.

## STRATEGIC POSTURE

Any good strategy requires a choice about strategic posture. Fundamentally, *posture* defines the intent of a strategy relative to the current and future state of an industry. (See figure "The Three Strategic Postures.") *Shapers* aim to drive their industries toward a new structure of their own devising. Their strategies are about creating new opportunities in a market—either by shaking up relatively stable level 1 industries or by trying to control the direction of the market in industries with higher levels of uncertainty. Kodak, for example, through its investment in digital photography, is pursuing a shaping strategy in an effort to maintain its leadership position, as a new technology supersedes the one currently generating most of its earnings. Although its product technology is new, Kodak's strategy is still based on a traditional model in which the company provides digital cameras and film while photo-processing stores provide many of the photo-printing and storage functions for the consumer. Hewlett-Packard also seeks

---

### The Three Strategic Postures

 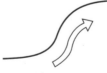 

| **Shape the future** | **Adapt to the future** | **Reserve the right to play** |
|---|---|---|
| Play a leadership role in establishing how the industry operates, for example: <br> – setting standards <br> – creating demand | Win through speed, agility, and flexibility in recognizing and capturing opportunities in existing markets | Invest sufficiently to stay in the game but avoid premature commitments |

to be a shaper in this market, but it is pursuing a radically different model in which high-quality, low-cost photo printers shift photo processing from stores to the home.

In contrast, *adapters* take the current industry structure and its future evolution as givens, and they react to the opportunities the market offers. In environments with little uncertainty, adapters choose a strategic positioning—that is, where and how to compete—in the current industry. At higher levels of uncertainty, their strategies are predicated on the ability to recognize and respond quickly to market developments. In the highly volatile telecommunications-service industry, for example, service resellers are adapters. They buy and resell the latest products and services offered by the major telecom providers, relying on pricing and effective execution rather than on product innovation as their source of competitive advantage.

The third strategic posture, *reserving the right to play*, is a special form of adapting. This posture is relevant only in levels 2 through 4; it involves making incremental investments today that put a company in a privileged position, through either superior information, cost structures, or relationships between customers and suppliers. That allows the company to wait until the environment becomes less uncertain before formulating a strategy. Many pharmaceutical companies are reserving the right to play in the market for gene therapy applications by acquiring or allying with small biotech firms that have relevant expertise. Providing privileged access to the latest industry developments, these are low-cost investments compared with building a proprietary, internal gene-therapy R&D program.

## A PORTFOLIO OF ACTIONS

A posture is not a complete strategy. It clarifies strategic intent but not the actions required to fulfill that intent. Three types of moves are especially relevant to implementing strategy under conditions of uncertainty: big bets, options, and no-regrets moves. (See figure "What's in a Portfolio of Actions?")

*Big bets* are large commitments, such as major capital investments or acquisitions, that will result in large payoffs in some scenarios and large losses in others. Not surprisingly, shaping strategies usually involve big bets, whereas adapting and reserving the right to play do not.

*Options* are designed to secure the big payoffs of the best-case scenarios while minimizing losses in the worst-case scenarios. This asymmetric payoff structure makes them resemble financial options. Most options involve making modest initial investments that will allow companies to ramp up or scale back the investment later as the market evolves. Classic examples include conducting pilot trials before the full-scale intro-

---

### What's in a Portfolio of Actions?

*These building blocks are distinguished by three payoff profiles—that is, the amount of investment required up front and the conditions under which the investment will yield a positive return.*

| Scenario | Value |
|----------|-------|
| 1. | + |
| 2. | + |
| 3. | + |
| 4. | + |

**No-regrets moves**

Strategic decisions that have positive payoffs in any scenario

**Options**

Decisions that yield a significant positive payoff in some outcomes and a (small) negative effect in others

**Big bets**

Focused strategies with positive payoffs in one or more scenarios but a negative effect in others

duction of a new product, entering into limited joint ventures for distribution to minimize the risk of breaking into new markets, and licensing an alternative technology in case it proves to be superior to a current technology. Those reserving the right to play rely heavily on options, but shapers use them as well, either to shape an emerging but uncertain market as an early mover or to hedge their big bets.

Finally, *no-regrets moves* are just that—moves that will pay off no matter what happens. Managers often focus on obvious no-regrets moves like initiatives aimed at reducing costs, gathering competitive intelligence, or building skills. However, even in highly uncertain environments, strategic decisions like investing in capacity and entering certain markets can be no-regrets moves. Whether or not they put a name to them, most managers understand intuitively that no-regrets moves are an essential element of any strategy.

The choice of a strategic posture and an accompanying portfolio of actions sounds straightforward. But in practice, these decisions are highly dependent on the level of uncertainty facing a given business. Thus the four-level framework can help clarify the practical implications implicit in any choice of strategic posture and actions. The discussion that follows will demonstrate the different strategic challenges that each level of uncertainty poses and how the portfolio of actions may be applied.

## STRATEGY IN LEVEL 1'S CLEAR-ENOUGH FUTURE

In predictable business environments, most companies are adapters. Analysis is designed to predict an industry's future landscape, and strategy involves making positioning choices about where and how to compete. When the underlying analysis is sound, such strategies are by definition made up of a series of no-regrets moves.

Adapter strategies in level 1 situations are not necessarily incremental or boring. For example, Southwest Airlines Company's no-frills, point-to-point service is a highly innovative, value-creating adapter strategy, as was Gateway 2000's low-cost assembly and direct-mail distribution strategy when it entered the personal computer market in the late 1980s. In both cases, managers were able to identify unexploited opportunities in relatively low-uncertainty environments within the existing market structure. The best level 1 adapters create value through innovations in their products or services or through improvements in their business systems without otherwise fundamentally changing the industry.

It is also possible to be a shaper in level 1 situations, but that is risky and rare, since level 1 shapers increase the amount of residual uncertainty in an otherwise predictable market—for themselves and their competitors—in an attempt to fundamentally alter long-standing industry structures and conduct. Consider Federal Express Corporation's overnight-delivery strategy. When it entered the mail-and-package delivery industry, a stable level 1 situation, FedEx's strategy in effect created level 3 uncertainty for itself. That is, even though CEO Frederick W. Smith commissioned detailed consulting reports that confirmed the feasibility of his business concept, only a broad range of potential demand for overnight services could be identified at the time. For the industry incumbents like United Parcel Service, FedEx created level 2 uncertainty. FedEx's move raised two questions for UPS: Will the overnight-delivery strategy succeed or not? and Will UPS have to offer a similar service to remain a viable competitor in the market?

Over time, the industry returned to level 1 stability, but with a fundamentally new structure. FedEx's bet paid off, forcing the rest of the industry to adapt to the new demand for overnight services.

What portfolio of actions did it take to realize that strategy? Like most shaper strategies, even in level 1 situations, this one required some big bets. That said, it often makes sense to build options into a shaper strategy to hedge against bad bets. Smith might have hedged his bets by leasing existing cargo airplanes instead of purchasing and retrofitting his original fleet of Falcon "minifreighters," or he could have outsourced ground pickup and delivery services. Such moves would have limited the amount of capital he would have needed to sink into his new strategy and facilitated a graceful exit had his concept failed. However, that kind of insurance doesn't always come cheap. In FedEx's case, had Smith leased standard-size cargo planes, he would have come under the restrictive regulations of the Civil Aeronautics Board. And outsourcing local pickups and deliveries would have diluted FedEx's unique door-to-door value to customers. Thus Smith stuck mainly to big bets in implementing his strategy, which drove him to the brink of bankruptcy in his first two years of operation but ultimately reshaped an entire industry.

## STRATEGY IN LEVEL 2´S ALTERNATE FUTURES

If shapers in level 1 try to raise uncertainty, in levels 2 through 4 they try to lower uncertainty and create order out of chaos. In level 2, a shaping strategy is designed to increase the probability that a favored industry scenario will occur. A shaper in a capital-intensive industry like pulp and paper, for example, wants to prevent competitors from creating excess capacity that would destroy the industry's profitability. Consequently, shapers in such cases might commit their companies to building new capacity far in advance of an upturn in demand to preempt the competition, or they might consolidate the industry through mergers and acquisitions.

Consider the Microsoft Network (MSN). A few years ago, one could identify a discrete set of possible ways in which transactions would be conducted between networked computers. Either proprietary networks such as MSN would become the standard, or open networks like the Internet would prevail. Uncertainty in this situation was thus at level 2, even though other related strategy issues—such as determining the level of consumer demand for networked applications—were level 3 problems.

Microsoft could reasonably expect to shape the way markets for electronic commerce evolved if it created the proprietary MSN network. It would, in effect, be building a commerce hub that would link both suppliers and consumers through the MSN gateway. The strategy was a big bet: the development costs were significant and, more important, involved an enormously high level of industry exposure and attention. In effect, for Microsoft, it constituted a big credibility bet. Microsoft's activities in other areas—such as including one-button access to

*Shaping strategies can fail, so the best companies supplement their shaping bets with options that let them change course quickly.*

MSN from Windows95—were designed to increase the probability that this shaping bet would pay off.

But even the best shapers must be prepared to adapt. In the battle between proprietary and open networks, certain trigger variables—growth in the number of Internet and MSN subscribers, for example, or the activity profiles of early MSN subscribers—could provide valuable insight into how the market was evolving. When it became clear that open networks would prevail, Microsoft refocused the MSN concept around the Internet. Microsoft's shift illustrates that choices of strategic posture are not carved in stone, and it underscores the value of maintaining strategic flexibility under uncertainty. Shaping strategies can fail, so the best companies supplement their shaping bets with options that allow them to change course quickly if necessary. Microsoft was able to do just that because it remained flexible by being willing to cut its losses, by building a cadre of engineers who had a wide range of general-programming and product-development skills, and by closely monitoring key trigger variables. In uncertain environments, it is a mistake to let strategies run on autopilot, remaining content to update them only through standard year-end strategy reviews.

Because trigger variables are often relatively simple to monitor in level 2, it can be easy to adapt or reserve the right to play. For instance, companies that generate electricity—and others whose business depends on energy-intensive production processes—often face level 2 uncertainty in determining the relative cost of different fuel alternatives. Discrete scenarios can often be identified—for example, either natural gas or oil will be the low-cost fuel. Many companies thus choose an adapter strategy when building new plants: they construct flexible manufacturing processes that can switch easily between different fuels.

Chemical companies often choose to reserve the right to play when facing level 2 uncertainty in predicting the performance of a new technology. If the technology performs well, companies will have to employ it to remain competitive in the market. But if it does not fulfill its promise, incumbents can compete effectively with existing technologies. Most companies are reluctant to bet several hundred million dollars on building new capacity and retrofitting old plants around a new technology until it is proven. But if they don't make at least incremental investments in the short run, they risk falling too far behind competitors should the technology succeed. Thus many will purchase options to license the new technology within a specified time frame or begin retrofitting a proportion of existing capacity around the new technology. In either case, small, up-front commitments give the companies privileged positions, but not obligations, to ramp up or discontinue development of the new technology as its performance attributes become clearer over time.

## STRATEGY IN LEVEL 3'S RANGE OF FUTURES

Shaping takes a different form in level 3. If at level 2, shapers are trying to make a discrete outcome occur, at level 3, they are trying to move the market in a general direction because they can identify only a range of possible outcomes. Consider the battle over standards for electronic cash transactions, currently a level 3 problem since one can define a range of potential products and services that fall between purely paper-based and purely electronic cash transactions, but it is unclear today whether there are any natural discrete scenarios within that range. Mondex International, a consortium of financial services providers and technology companies, is attempting to shape the future by establishing what it hopes will become universal electronic-cash standards. Its shaping posture is backed by big-bet investments in product development, infrastructure, and pilot experiments to speed customer acceptance.

In contrast, regional banks are mainly choosing adapter strategies. An adapter posture at uncertainty levels 3 or 4 is often achieved primarily through investments in organizational capabilities designed to keep options open. Because they must make and implement strategy choices in real time, adapters need quick access to the best market information and the most flexible organizational structures. Many regional banks, for example, have put in place steering committees focused on electronic payments, R&D projects, and competitive-intelligence systems so that they can constantly monitor developments in electronic payment technology and markets. (See figure "How a Regional Bank Confronts the Uncertainties in Electronic Commerce.") In addition, many regional banks are making small investments in industry consortia as another way to monitor events. This adapter approach makes sense for most regional banks—they don't have the deep pockets and skills necessary to set standards for the electronic payment market, yet it is essential that they be able to offer the latest electronic services to their customers as such services become available.

Reserving the right to play is a common posture in level 3. Consider a telecommunications company trying to decide whether to make a $1 billion investment in

# How a Regional Bank Confronts the Uncertainties in Electronic Commerce

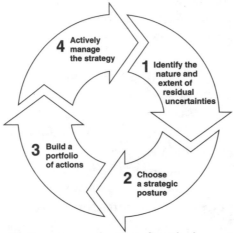

## 1. Identify the nature and extent of residual uncertainties

**Key areas of uncertainty include:**
- How much electronic commerce will occur on the Internet
- How quickly consumers will switch from paper-based to electronic payments
- Which specific instruments will become the primary payment vehicles (smart cards? E-cash?)
- What structure will emerge for the electronic commerce industry
- How vertically integrated most players will be
- What roles banks and nonbanks will play

**The bank is facing level 3 uncertainty in some areas and level 4 in others**

## 2. Choose a strategic posture

**Objectives:**
- Defend current customer franchise from attack by new technology-based competitors
- Capture new business opportunities in fast growing markets

**Overall posture: reserve the right to play**

## 3. Build a portfolio of actions

**Near-term opportunities to offer more innovative products in specific areas where the bank is strong (for example, procurement cards, industry-specific payment products) represent no-regrets moves.**

**Offering leading-edge payment products to high-value customer segments that are most vulnerable to attackers is another no-regrets move.**

**Forming a small new-business unit is a growth option to:**
- Conduct R&D for new payment ideas
- Monitor industry developments in the broad area of retail electronic payments

## 4. Actively manage the strategy

**Monitor key trigger events such as adoption rates for emerging products and the behavior of nontraditional competitors such as telephone companies.**

**Establish a short-cycle review of the portfolio of options.**

**Participate in a number of industry consortia to reduce uncertainty.**

broadband cable networks in the early 1990s. The decision hinged on level 3 uncertainties such as demand for interactive TV service. No amount of solid market research could precisely forecast consumer demand for services that didn't even exist yet. However, making incremental investments in broadband-network trials could provide useful information, and it would put the company in a privileged position to expand the business in the future should that prove attractive. By restructuring the broadband-investment decision from a big bet to a series of options, the company reserved the right to play in a potentially lucrative market without having to bet the farm or risk being preempted by a competitor.

### STRATEGY IN LEVEL 4´S TRUE AMBIGUITY

Paradoxically, even though level 4 situations contain the greatest uncertainty, they may offer higher returns and involve lower risks for companies seeking to shape the market than situations in either level 2 or 3. Recall that level 4 situations are transitional by nature, often occurring after a major technological, macroeconomic, or legislative shock. Since no player necessarily knows the best strategy in these environments, the shaper's role is to provide a vision of an industry structure and standards that will coordinate the strategies of other players and drive the market toward a more stable and favorable outcome.

Mahathir bin Mohamad, Malaysia's prime minister, is trying to shape the future of the multimedia industry in the Asian Pacific Rim. This is truly a level 4 strategy problem at this point. Potential products are undefined, as are the players, the level of customer demand, and the technology standards, among other factors. The government is trying to create order out of this chaos by investing at least $15 billion to create a so-called Multimedia Super Corridor (MSC) in Malaysia. The MSC is a 750-square-kilometer zone south of Kuala Lumpur that will include state-of-the-art "smart" buildings for software companies, regional headquarters for multinational corporations, a "Multimedia University," a paperless government center called Putrajaya, and a new city called Cyberjaya. By leveraging incentives like a ten-year exemption from the tax on profits, the MSC has received commitments from more than 40

*Netscape relied on its credibility, rather than its deep pockets, to shape Internet browser standards.*

Malaysian and foreign companies so far, including such powerhouses as Intel, Microsoft, Nippon Telegraph and Telephone, Oracle, and Sun Microsystems. Mahathir's shaping strategy is predicated on the notion that the MSC will create a web of relationships between content and hardware providers that will result in clear industry standards and a set of complementary multimedia products and services. Intel's Malaysia managing director, David B. Marsing, recognized Mahathir's shaping aspirations when he noted, "If you're an evolutionist, it's strange. They're [the Malaysian government] trying to intervene instead of letting it evolve."

Shapers need not make enormous bets as the Malaysian government is doing to be successful in level 3 or 4 situations, however. All that is required is the credibility to coordinate the strategies of different players around the preferred outcome. Netscape Communications Corporation, for example, didn't rely on deep pockets to shape Internet browser standards. Instead, it leveraged the credibility of its leadership team in the industry so that other industry players thought, "If these guys think this is the way to go, they must be right."

Reserving the right to play is common, but potentially dangerous, in level 4 situations. Oil companies believed they were reserving the right to compete in China by buying options to establish various beachheads there some 20 years ago. However, in such level 4 situations, it is extremely difficult to determine whether incremental investments are truly reserving the right to play or simply the right to lose. A few general rules apply. First, look for a high degree of leverage. If the choice of beachhead in China comes down to maintaining a small, but expensive, local operation or developing a limited joint venture with a local distributor, all else being equal, go for the low-cost option. Higher-cost options must be justified with explicit arguments for why they would put the company in a better position to ramp up over time. Second, don't get locked into one position through neglect. Options should be rigorously reevaluated whenever important uncertainties are clarified—at least every six months. Remember, level 4 situations are transitional, and most will quickly move toward levels 3 and 2.

The difficulty of managing options in level 4 situations often drives players toward adapter postures. As in level 3, an adapter posture in level 4 is frequently implemented by making investments in organizational capabilities. Most potential players in the multimedia industry are adopting that posture today but will soon be making bigger bets as the industry moves into level 3 and 2 uncertainty over time.

## A New Approach to Uncertainty

At the heart of the traditional approach to strategy lies the assumption that by applying a set of powerful analytic tools, executives can predict the future of any business accurately enough to allow them to choose a clear strategic direction. In relatively stable businesses, that approach continues to work well. But it tends to break down when the environment is so uncertain that no amount of good analysis will allow them to predict the future.

Levels of uncertainty regularly confronting managers today are so high that they need a new way to think about strategy. (See "Needed: A More Comprehensive Strategy Tool Kit," below.) The approach we've outlined will help executives avoid dangerous binary views of uncertainty. It offers a discipline for thinking rigorously and systematically about uncertainty. On one plane, it is a guide to judging which analytic tools can help in making decisions at various levels of uncertainty and which cannot. On a broader plane, our framework is a way to tackle the most challenging decisions that executives have to make, offering a more complete and sophisticated understanding of the uncertainty they face and its implications for strategy.

---

## Needed: A More Comprehensive Strategy Tool Kit

IN ORDER TO PERFORM THE KINDS OF ANALYSES APPROPRIATE TO HIGH LEVELS OF UNCERTAINTY, many companies will need to supplement their standard strategy tool kit. Scenario-planning techniques are fundamental to determining strategy under conditions of uncertainty. Game theory will help managers understand uncertainties based on competitors' conduct. Systems dynamics and agent-based simulation models can help in understanding the complex interactions in the market. Real-options valuation models can help in correctly valuing investments in learning and flexibility. The following sources will help managers get started:

- **Scenario Planning.** Kees van der Heijden, *Scenarios: The Art of Strategic Conversation* (New York: John Wiley & Sons, 1996); Paul J.H. Schoemaker, "Scenario Planning: A New Tool for Strategic Thinking," *Sloan Management Review,* Winter 1995.

- **Game Theory.** Avinash K. Dixit and Barry J. Nalebuff, *Thinking Strategically: The Competitive Edge in Business, Politics, and Everyday Life* (New York: W.W. Norton, 1991); Adam M. Brandenburger and Barry J. Nalebuff, "The Right Game: Use Game Theory to Shape Strategy," HBR July–August 1995.

- **System Dynamics.** Peter N. Senge, *Fifth Discipline: The Art and Practice of the Learning Organization* (New York: Doubleday, 1990); Arie de Geus, "Planning as Learning," HBR March–April 1988.

- **Agent-Based Models.** John L. Casti, *Would-Be Worlds: How Simulation Is Changing the Frontiers of Science* (New York: John Wiley & Sons, 1997).

- **Real Options.** Avinash K. Dixit and Robert S. Pindyck, "The Options Approach to Capital Investment," HBR May–June 1995; Timothy A. Luehrman, "What's It Worth?" HBR May–June 1997.

**Originally Published in November–December 1997**
**Reprint 97603**

*This article is based on research sponsored by McKinsey's ongoing Strategy Theory Initiative (STI). The authors would like to thank their STI colleagues for their significant contributions to this article.*

# Competing for the Future

GARY HAMEL AND

C. K. PRAHALAD

## Executive Summary

IS YOUR COMPANY A RULE MAKER OR A RULE FOL-
LOWER? Does your company focus on catching up or
on getting out in front? Do you spend the bulk of your
time as a maintenance engineer preserving the status
quo or as an architect designing the future? Difficult
questions like these go unanswered not because senior
managers are lazy—most are working harder than ever—
but because they won't admit that they are less than fully
in control of their companies' future. In this adaptation
from their upcoming book, Hamel and Prahalad urge
senior managers to look toward and ponder their ability
to shape their companies in the years and decades to
come.

If the future is not occupying senior managers, what
is? Restructuring and reengineering. While both are legitimate tasks, they have more to do with shoring up today's

33

businesses than with building tomorrow's industries. Restructuring tries to correct the mistakes of the past; reengineering mostly involves catching up to competitors.

Creating the future, as Electronic Data Systems has done, for example, requires industry foresight. Since change is inevitable, managers must decide whether it will happen in a crisis atmosphere or in a calm and considered manner, with foresight about the future of the industry; whether the agenda for change will be set by a company's unique point of view about the future or by its more prescient competitors. Too often, profound thinking about the future occurs only when present success has been eroded. To get ahead of the industry change curve, senior managers must recognize that the real focus for their companies is the chance to compete for the future.

---

Look around your company. Look at the high-profile initiatives that have recently been launched, the issues preoccupying senior management, the criteria and benchmarks by which progress is measured, your track record of new-business creation. Look into the faces of your colleagues, and consider their ambitions and fears. Look toward the future, and ponder your company's ability to shape that future in the years and decades to come.

Now ask yourself: Do senior managers in my company have a clear and shared understanding of how the industry may be different ten years from now? Is my company's point of view about the future unique among competitors?

These are not rhetorical questions. Get a pencil and score your company.

**How does senior management's point of view about the future compare with that of your competitors?**

Conventional ........................... Distinctive
and reactive                              and farsighted

**Which business issue absorbs more senior-management attention?**

Reengineering ........................ Regenerating
core processes                          core strategies

**How do competitors view your company?**

Mostly as a ........................... Mostly as a
rule follower                           rule maker

**What is your company's strength?**

Operational ............................ Innovation
efficiency                              and growth

**What is the focus of your company's advantage-building efforts?**

Mostly ............................... Mostly getting
catching up                            out in front

**What has set your transformation agenda?**

Our competitors ..................... Our foresight

**Do you spend the bulk of your time as a maintenance engineer preserving the status quo or as an architect designing the future?**

Mostly as ............................ Mostly as
an engineer                          an architect

   If your scores fall somewhere in the middle or off to the left, your company may be devoting too much energy to preserving the past and not enough to creating the future.

When we talk to senior managers about competing for the future, we ask them three questions. First, what percentage of your time is spent on external rather than internal issues—on understanding, for example, the implications of a particular new technology instead of debating corporate overhead allocations? Second, of this time spent looking outward, how much do you spend considering how the world may change in five or ten years rather than worrying about winning the next big contract or responding to a competitor's pricing move? Third, of the time devoted to looking outward *and* forward, how much do you spend working with colleagues to build a deeply shared, well-tested perspective on the future as opposed to a personal and idiosyncratic view?

The answers to these questions typically conform to what we call the "40/30/20 Rule." In our experience, about 40% of a senior executive's time is devoted to looking outward and, of this time, about 30% is spent peering three, four, five, or more years into the future. Of that time spent looking forward, no more than 20% is devoted to building a collective view of the future (the other 80% is spent considering the future of the manager's particular business). Thus, on average, senior managers devote less than 3% (40% $\times$ 30% $\times$ 20%) of their time to building a *corporate* perspective on the future. In some companies, the figure is less than 1%. Our experience suggests that to develop a distinctive point of view about the future, senior managers must be willing to devote considerably more of their time. And after the initial burst of energy that they must expend to develop a distinct view of the future, managers must be willing to adjust that perspective as the future unfolds.

Such commitment as well as substantial and sustained intellectual energy is required to answer such questions as: What new core competencies will we need to build? What new product concepts should we pioneer? What alliances will we need to form? What nascent development programs should we protect? What long-term regulatory initiatives should we pursue?

We believe such questions have received far too little attention in many companies, not because senior managers are lazy—most are working harder than ever—but because they won't admit, to themselves or to their employees, that they are less than fully in control of their companies' future. Difficult questions go unanswered because they challenge the assumption that top management really is in control, really does have more accurate foresight

*When faced with a competitiveness problem, most executives undertake emergency-room surgery, carving away corporate fat and amputating underperforming businesses.*

than anyone else in the corporation, and already has a clear and compelling view of the company's future. Senior managers are often unwilling to confront these illusions. So the urgent drives out the important; the future is left largely unexplored; and the capacity to act, rather than to think and imagine, becomes the sole measure of leadership.

## Beyond Restructuring

The painful upheavals in so many companies in recent years reflect the failure of one-time industry leaders to keep up with the accelerating pace of industry change.

For decades, the changes undertaken at Sears, General Motors, IBM, Westinghouse, Volkswagen, and other incumbents were, if not exactly glacial in speed, more or less linear extrapolations of the past. Those companies were run by managers, not leaders, by maintenance engineers, not architects.

If the future is not occupying senior managers, what is? Restructuring and reengineering. While both are legitimate and important tasks, they have more to do with shoring up today's businesses than with building tomorrow's industries. Any company that is a bystander on the road to the future will watch its structure, values, and skills become progressively less attuned to industry realities. Such a discrepancy between the pace of industrial change and the pace of company change gives rise to the need for organizational transformation.

A company's organizational transformation agenda typically includes downsizing, overhead reduction, employee empowerment, process redesign, and portfolio rationalization. When a competitiveness problem (stagnant growth, declining margins, and falling market share, for example) can no longer be ignored, most executives pick up a knife and begin the painful work of restructuring. The goal is to carve away layers of corporate fat and amputate underperforming businesses. Executives who don't have the stomach for emergency-room surgery, like John Akers at IBM or Robert Stempel at GM, soon find themselves out of a job.

*Most layoffs at large companies have been the fault of managers who fell asleep at the wheel and missed the turnoff for the future.*

Masquerading behind terms like refocusing, delayering, decluttering, and right-sizing (Why is the "right" size always smaller?), restructuring always results in fewer employees. In 1993, large U.S. companies announced nearly 600,000 layoffs—25% more than were announced in 1992 and nearly 10% more than in 1991, the year in which the U.S. recession hit its lowest point. While European companies have long tried to put off their own day of reckoning, bloated payrolls and out-of-control employment costs have made downsizing as inevitable in the old world as it is in the new. Despite excuses about global competition and the impact of productivity-enhancing technology, most layoffs at large U.S. companies have been the fault of senior managers who fell asleep at the wheel and missed the turnoff for the future.

With no growth or slow growth, companies soon find it impossible to support their burgeoning employment rosters and traditional R&D budgets and investment programs. The problems of low growth are often compounded by inattentiveness to ballooning overheads (IBM's problem), diversification into unrelated businesses (Xerox's foray into financial services), and the paralysis imposed by an unfailingly conservative staff. It is not surprising that shareholders are giving moribund companies unequivocal marching orders: "Make this company lean and mean;" "Make the assets sweat;" "Get back to basics." In most companies, return on capital employed, shareholder value, and revenue per employee have become the primary arbiters of top-management performance.

Although perhaps inescapable and in many cases commendable, restructuring has destroyed lives, homes, and communities in the name of efficiency and produc-

tivity. While it is impossible to argue with such objectives, pursuing them single-mindedly does the cause of
competitiveness as much harm as good. Let us explain.

Imagine a CEO who is fully aware that if he or she
doesn't make effective use of corporate resources, someone else will be given the chance. So the chief executive
launches a tough program to improve return on investment. Now, ROI (or return on net assets or return on
capital employed) has two components: a numerator—
net income—and a denominator—investment, net
assets, or capital employed. (In a service industry, a
more appropriate denominator may be head count.)
Managers know that raising net income is likely to be
harder than cutting assets and head count. To increase
the numerator, top management must have a sense of
where new opportunities lie, must be able to anticipate
changing customer needs, must have invested in building new competencies, and so on. So under intense pressure for a quick ROI improvement, executives reach for
the lever that will bring the fastest, surest result: the
denominator.

The United States and Britain have produced an
entire generation of managers obsessed with denomina-
tors. They can downsize, declutter, delayer, and divest
better than any other managers. Even before the current
wave of downsizing, U.S. and British companies had, on
average, the highest asset-productivity ratios of any
companies in the world. Denominator management is
an accountant's shortcut to asset productivity.

Don't misunderstand. A company must get to the
future not only first but also for less. But there is more
than one route to productivity improvement. Just as any
company that cuts the denominator and maintains revenues will reap productivity gains, so too will any com-

pany that succeeds in increasing its revenue stream atop a slower-growing or constant capital and employment base. Although the first approach may be necessary, we believe the second is usually more desirable.

In a world in which competitors are capable of achieving 5%, 10%, or 15% real growth in revenues, aggressive denominator reduction under a flat revenue stream is simply a way to sell market share and the future of the company. Marketing strategists term this a *harvest strategy* and consider it a no-brainer. Between 1969 and 1991, for example, Britain's manufacturing output (the numerator) went up by only 10% in real terms. Yet over this same period, the number of people employed in British manufacturing (the denominator) was nearly halved. The result was that during the early and mid-1980s, the Thatcher years, British manufacturing productivity increased faster than that of any other major industrialized country except Japan. Though Britain's financial press and Conservative ministers trumpeted this as a "success," it was, of course, bittersweet. While new legislation limited the power of trade unions, and the liberalization of statutory impediments to workforce reduction enabled management to excise inefficient and outmoded work practices, British companies demonstrated scant ability to create new markets at home and abroad. In effect, British companies surrendered global market share. One almost expected to pick up the *Financial Times* and find that Britain had finally matched Japan's manufacturing productivity—and that the last remaining person at work in British manufacturing was the most productive son of a gun on the planet.

The social costs of such denominator-driven job losses are high. Although an individual company may be able to avoid some of those costs, society cannot. In Britain, the service sector could not absorb all the displaced manufacturing workers and underwent its own vicious downsizing in the recession that began in 1989. Downsizing also causes employee morale to plummet. What employees hear is that "people are our most important asset." What they see is that people are the most expendable asset.

Moreover, restructuring seldom results in fundamental business improvements. At best, it buys time. One study of 16 large U.S. companies with at least three years of restructuring experience found that while restructuring usually did raise a company's share price, such improvement was almost always temporary. Three years into restructuring, the share prices of the companies surveyed were, on average, lagging even further behind index growth rates than they had been when the restructuring effort began.

## Beyond Reengineering

Downsizing attempts to correct the mistakes of the past, not to create the markets of the future. But getting smaller is not enough. Recognizing that restructuring is a dead end, smart companies move on to reengineering. The difference between restructuring and reengineering is that the latter offers at least the hope, if not always the reality, of getting better as well as getting leaner. Yet in many companies, reengineering is more about catching up than getting out in front.

For example, Detroit automakers are catching up with Japanese rivals on quality and cost. Supplier networks have been reconstituted, product-development processes redesigned, and manufacturing processes reengineered. However, the cheerful headlines heralding Detroit's comeback miss the deeper story—among the losses have been hundreds of thousands of jobs, 20-some percentage points of market share in the United States, and any hope of U.S. automakers beating Japanese rivals in the booming Asian markets anytime soon.

Catching up is not enough. In a survey taken at the end of the 1980s, nearly 80% of U.S. managers polled believed that quality would be a fundamental source of competitive advantage in the year 2000, but barely half of Japanese managers agreed. Their primary goal was to create new products and businesses.[1] Does this mean that Japanese managers will turn their backs on quality? Of course not. It merely indicates that by the year 2000, quality will be the price of market entry, not a competitive differentiator. Japanese managers realize that tomorrow's competitive advantages will be different from today's. It remains to be seen whether Detroit will set the pace in the next round of competition and produce vehicles as exciting as they are fuel efficient and reliable or will once again rest on its laurels.

We come across far too many top managers whose advantage-building agenda is still dominated by quality, time-to-market, and customer responsiveness. While such advantages are prerequisites for survival, they are hardly a testimony to management foresight. Though managers often try to make a virtue out of imitation, dressing it up in the fashionable colors of "adaptiveness," what they are adapting to all too often are the preemptive strategies of more imaginative competitors.

Consider Xerox. During the 1970s and 1980s, Xerox surrendered a substantial amount of market share to

Japanese competitors, such as Canon and Sharp. Recognizing that the company was on the slippery slope to oblivion, Xerox benchmarked its competitors and fundamentally reengineered its processes. By the early 1990s, the company had become a textbook example of how to reduce costs, improve quality, and satisfy customers. But amid all the talk of the new "American Samurai," two issues were overlooked. First, although Xerox halted the erosion of its market share, it has not fully recaptured share lost to its Japanese competitors: Canon remains one of the largest copier manufacturers in the world. Second, despite pioneering research in laser printing, networking, icon-based computing, and the laptop computer, Xerox has not created any substantial new businesses outside its copier core. Although Xerox may have invented the office as we know it today and as it's likely to be, the company has actually profited very little from its creation.

In fact, Xerox has probably left more money on the table, in the form of underexploited innovation, than any other company in history. Why? Because to create new businesses, Xerox would have had to regenerate its core strategy: the way it defined its market, its distribution channels, its customers, its competitors, the criteria for promoting managers, the metrics used to measure success, and so on. A company surrenders today's businesses when it gets smaller faster than it gets better. A company surrenders tomorrow's businesses when it gets better without changing.

*If managers don't have detailed answers to questions about the future, their companies can't expect to be market leaders.*

We meet many managers who describe their companies as "market leaders." (With enough creativity in delimiting market boundaries, almost any company can claim to be a market leader.) But market leadership today certainly doesn't equal market leadership tomorrow. Think about two sets of questions:

| Today | In the Future |
|---|---|
| Which customers do you serve today? | Which customers will you serve in the future? |
| Through what channels do you reach customers today? | Through what channels will you reach customers in the future? |
| Who are your competitors today? | Who will your competitors be in the future? |
| What is the basis for your competitive advantage today? | What will be the basis for your competitive advantage in the future? |
| Where do your margins come from today? | Where will your margins come from in the future? |
| What skills or capabilities make you unique today? | What skills or capabilities will make you unique in the future? |

If senior executives don't have reasonably detailed answers to the "future" questions, and if the answers they have are not significantly different from the "today" answers, there is little chance that their companies will remain market leaders. The market a company dominates today is likely to change substantially over the next ten years. There's no such thing as "sustaining" leadership; it must be regenerated again and again.

## Creating the Future

Organizational transformation must be driven by a point of view about the future of the industry: How do we want this industry to be shaped in five or ten years? What must we do to ensure that the industry evolves in a way that is maximally advantageous for us? What skills and capabilities must we begin building now if we are to occupy the industry high ground in the future? How should we organize for opportunities that may not fit neatly within the boundaries of current business units and divisions? Since most companies don't start with a shared view of the future, seniors managers' first task is to develop a process for pulling together the collective wisdom within an organization. Concern for the future, a sense of where opportunities lie, and an understanding of organizational change are not the province of any group; people from all levels of a company can help define the future.

One company that developed a process for establishing a point of view about the future is Electronic Data Systems (EDS), based in Plano, Texas. In 1992, EDS's position seemed unassailable. With $8.2 billion in sales, EDS had recorded its thirtieth consecutive year of record earnings and looked forward to the ever-growing demand for computer-services outsourcing. EDS expected to become at least a $25 billion company by the year 2000.

But some top executives, including Chairman Lester Alberthal, foresaw problems. Margins were under intense pressure from new competitors, such as Andersen Consulting. Customers were demanding hefty discounts in their long-term service contracts. Fewer new customers could be found among leading-edge IT users in the United States. And future business needs would involve desktop computers, not the mainframes EDS specialized in, while the most exciting new information-network services would focus on the home, not the office.

The company's top officers, known as the Leadership Council, concluded that EDS was no more immune from "great company disease" than any other successful enterprise. Council members committed themselves to rebuilding industry leadership for the 1990s and beyond.

As it happened, others in the company were already thinking along similar lines. Back in 1990, a small band of EDS managers, none of them yet corporate officers, had created a Corporate Change Team. Despite their lack of an official charter, team members believed EDS needed to rethink its direction and its deepest assumptions. They soon realized this would require far more resources, both temporal and intellectual, than could be mustered by one small team.

After talking with the Leadership Council about its goals, the Corporate Change Team developed a unique approach to company renewal. From across the company and around the world, 150 EDS managers—key resource holders as well as less-senior managers who were known to be challenging, bright, and unconventional—gathered in Dallas, 30 at a time, to begin creating the future. Each of the five "waves" considered in detail the economic threats to EDS and the opportunities afforded by the digital revolution. Each wave was given an assignment. The first wave studied the discontinuities that EDS could use to change the shape of the industry. The second and third waves tried to develop a view of the company's competencies that was substantially independent from current definitions of EDS's served markets. They then benchmarked those competencies against EDS's strongest competitors. Drawing on the work of the previous waves, wave four explored opportunities on the horizon. And wave five considered how to devote more company resources to building competencies and developing opportunities.

Each wave's output was thoroughly debated by the other waves and with the Leadership Council. Finally, a team composed of members from all the waves produced a draft corporate strategy, which, again, was debated throughout the company.

EDS's new strategy is captured in three words: globalize, informationalize, and individualize. The strategy is based on the company's ability to use information technology to span geographical, cultural, and organizational boundaries; to help customers convert data into information, information into knowledge, and knowledge into action; and to mass-customize and enable individuals to mass-customize information services and products.

The process of developing this strategy for the future was full of frustrations, surprises, unexpected insights, and missed deadlines. More than 2,000 people participated in the creation of EDS's new strategy, and nearly 30,000 person-hours were devoted to the exercise. (More than one-third of the time investment was made outside the company's normal business hours.)

EDS emerged from the process with a view of its industry and its role that was substantially broader, more creative, and more prescient than it had been 12 months earlier. This view was held not only by a few technical gurus or corporate visionaries but by every senior EDS manager. Indeed, those who participated in the process thought it contributed as much to leadership development as it did to strategy development.

## The Quest for Foresight

To create the future as EDS has done requires industry foresight. Why do we talk of foresight rather than vision? Vision connotes a dream or an apparition, and there is more to industry foresight than a blinding flash of insight. Industry foresight is based on deep insights into trends in technology, demographics, regulations, and lifestyles, which can be harnessed to rewrite industry rules and create new competitive space. While understanding the potential implications of such trends requires creativity and imagination, any "vision" that is not based on a solid foundation is likely to be fantastical.

For this reason, industry foresight is a synthesis of many people's visions. Often, journalists or sycophantic employees have described foresight as the "vision" of one person. Much of the credit for NEC's visionary concept of "computers and communication" may have gone to Akira Kobayashi, but the idea of exploiting the convergence between the two industries synthesized the thinking of many in the company. Senior executives are not the only ones with industry foresight. In fact, their primary role is to capture and exploit the foresight that exists throughout the organization.

GIVEN THAT CHANGE IS INEVITABLE, the real issue for managers is whether that change will happen belatedly, in a crisis atmosphere, or with foresight, in a calm and considered manner; whether the transformation agenda will be set by a company's more prescient competitors or by its own point of view; whether transformation will be spasmodic and brutal or continuous and peaceful. Palace coups make great press copy, but the real objective is a transformation that is revolutionary in result and evolutionary in execution.

Developing a point of view about the future should be an ongoing project sustained by continuous debate within a company, not a massive one-time effort. Unfortunately, most companies consider the need to regenerate their strategies and reinvent their industries only when restructuring and reengineering fail to halt the process of corporate decline. To get ahead of the industry change curve, to have the chance of conducting a bloodless revolution, top managers must recognize that the real focus for their companies is the opportunity to compete for the future.

## Note

1. Donald Hambrick, *Reinventing the CEO: 21st Century Report* (New York: Korn Ferry International and the Columbia University Graduate School of Business, 1989).

**Originally published in July–August 1994**
**Reprint 94403**

*This article is adapted from* Competing for the Future, *published by Harvard Business School Press in September 1994.*

# Planning as Learning

ARIE P. DE GEUS

## Executive Summary

LONG-LIVED COMPANIES ADAPT themselves to the
business environment. They develop when times are
good and switch to a survival mode when times are turbulent. And they are successful at it because they have
senior executives who learn quickly and act effectively
as individuals and as a team.

Most management teams incorporate new information more slowly than the members do on their own.
Hearing a new signal, digesting it, confirming it, acting
on it—each step takes time. Too much time when the ability to learn faster than comnpetitors is the only real sustainable advantage. That's why, at Shell, planning is
about speeding up the learning process, not about making plans.

Lengthy lectures from planners seldom convince
experienced executives that they need to change the

way they think about their markets, competitors, and
business. Changing or suspending the corporate rules
works a lot better. So do games and serious play.
What-if scenarios, computer modeling, and interaction
with consultants are among the methods Shell uses to
help operating managers stay in tune with an inconsistent world.

---

Some years ago, the planning group at Shell[1] surveyed 30 companies that had been in business for
more than 75 years. What impressed us most was their
ability to live in harmony with the business environment, to switch from a survival mode when times were
turbulent to a self-development mode when the pace
of change was slow. And this pattern rang a familiar
bell because Shell's history is similarly replete with
switches from expansion to self-preservation and back
again to growth.

Early in our history, for example, there was a burst of
prosperity in the Far East and we dominated the market
for kerosene in tins and "oil for the lamps of China." Survival became the keynote, however, when Rockefeller's
Standard Oil snatched market share by cutting price. In
fact, it was the survival instinct that led in 1907 to the
joining of Royal Dutch Petroleum and the Shell Transport and Trading Company—separate businesses until
then and competitors in the Far East. This, in turn,
paved the way for Shell's expansion into the United
States in 1911 with a new product, Sumatran gasoline—
also a reaction to Standard Oil's activities.

Outcomes like these don't happen automatically. On
the contrary, they depend on the ability of a company's

senior managers to absorb what is going on in the business environment and to act on that information with appropriate business moves. In other words, they depend on learning. Or, more precisely, on institutional learning, which is the process whereby management teams change their shared mental models of their company, their markets, and their competitors. For this reason, we think of planning as learning and of corporate planning as institutional learning.

Institutional learning is much more difficult than individual learning. The high level of thinking among individual managers in most companies is admirable. And yet, the level of thinking that goes on in the management teams of most companies is considerably below the individual managers' capacities. In institutional learning situations, the learning level of the team is often the lowest common denominator, especially with teams that think of themselves as machines with mechanistic, specialized parts: the production manager looks at production, the distribution manager looks at distribution, the marketing manager looks at marketing.

Because high-level, effective, and continuous institutional learning and ensuing corporate change are the prerequisites for corporate success, we at Shell have asked ourselves two questions. How does a company learn and adapt? And, What is planning's role in corporate learning?

M Y ANSWER TO THE FIRST QUESTION, "how does a company learn and adapt," is that many do not or, at least, not very quickly. A full one-third of the *Fortune* "500" industrials listed in 1970 had vanished by 1983.

And W. Stewart Howe has pointed out in his 1986 book
*Corporate Strategy* that for every successful turnaround
there are two ailing companies that fail to recover. Yet
some companies obviously do learn and can adapt. In
fact, our survey identified several that were still vigorous
at 200, 300, and even 700 years of age. What made the
difference? Why are some companies better able to
adapt?

Sociologists and psychologists tell us it is pain that
makes people and living systems change. And certainly
corporations have their share of painful crises, the
recent spate of takeovers and takeover threats conspicu-
ously among them. But crisis management—pain management—is a dangerous way to manage for change.

Once in a crisis, everyone in the organization feels the
pain. The need for change is clear. The problem is that
you usually have little time and few options. The deeper
into the crisis you are, the fewer options remain. Crisis
management, by necessity, becomes autocratic management. The positive characteristic of a crisis is that the
decisions are quick. The other side of that coin is that
the implementation is rarely good; many companies fail
to survive.

The challenge, therefore, is to recognize and react to
environmental change before the pain of a crisis. Not
surprisingly, this is what the long-lived companies in our
study were so well able to do.

All these companies had a striking capacity to insti-
tutionalize change. They never stood still. Moreover,
they seemed to recognize that they had internal
strengths that could be developed as environmental conditions changed. Thus, Booker McConnell, founded in
1906 as a sugar company, developed shipping on the
back of its primary resource. British American Tobacco
recognized that marketing cigarettes was no different

from marketing perfume. Mitsubishi, founded in 1870 as a marine and trading company, acquired coal mines to secure access to ships' bunkers, built shipyards to repair imported ships, and developed a bank from the exchange business it had begun to finance shippers.

Changes like these grow out of a company's knowledge of itself and its environment. All managers have such knowledge and they develop it further all the time, since every living person—and system—is continuously engaged in learning. In fact, the normal decision process in corporations is a learning process, because people change their own mental models and build up a joint model as they talk. The problem is that the speed of that process is slow  too slow for a world in which the ability to learn faster than competitors may be the only sustainable competitive advantage.

Some five years ago, we had a good example of the time it takes for a message to be heard. One way in which we in Shell trigger institutional learning is through scenarios.[2] A certain set of scenarios gave our planners a clear signal that the oil industry, which had always been highly integrated, was so no longer. That contradicted all our existing models. High integration means that you are more or less in control of all the facets of your industry, so you can start optimizing. Optimization was the driving managerial model in Shell. What these scenarios essentially were saying was that we had to look for other management methods.

The first reaction from the organization was at best polite. There were few questions and no discussion. Some managers reacted critically: the scenarios were "basic theory that everyone already knew"; they had "little relevance to the realities of today's business." The message had been listened to but it had not yet been heard.

After a hiatus of some three months, people began asking lots of questions; a discussion started. The intervening months had provided time for the message to settle and for management's mental models to develop a few new hooks. Absorption, phase one of the learning process, had taken place.

During the next nine months, we moved through the other phases of the learning process. Operating executives at Shell incorporated this new information into their mental models of the business. They drew conclusions from the revised models and tested them against experience. Then, finally, they acted on the basis of the altered model. Hearing, digestion, confirmation, action: each step took time, its own sweet time.

In my experience this time span is typical. It will likely take 12 to 18 months from the moment a signal is received until it is acted on. The issue is not whether a company will learn, therefore, but whether it will learn fast and early. The critical question becomes, "Can we accelerate institutional learning?"

I am more and more persuaded that the answer to this question is yes. But before explaining why, I want to emphasize an important point about learning and the planner's role. The only relevant learning in a company is the learning done by those people who have the power to act (at Shell, the operating company management teams). So the real purpose of effective planning is not to make plans but to change the microcosm, the mental models that these decision makers carry in their heads. And this is what we at Shell and others elsewhere try to do.

In this role as facilitator, catalyst, and accelerator of the corporate learning process, planners are apt to fall into several traps. One is that we sometimes start with a mental model that is unrecognizable to our audience. Another is that we take too many steps at once. The third, and most serious, is that too often we communicate our information by teaching. This is a natural trap to fall into because it's what we've been conditioned to all our lives. But teaching, as John Holt points out, is actually one of the least efficient ways to convey knowledge.[3] At best, 40% of what is taught is received; in most situations, it is only about 25%.

It was a shock to learn how inefficient teaching is. Yet some reflection on our own experience drove the point home. After all, we had spent nearly 15 man-years preparing a set of scenarios which we then transmitted in a condensed version in $2^1/_2$ hours. Could we really have believed that our audience would understand all we were talking about?

Teaching has another disadvantage as well, especially in a business setting. Teachers must be given authority by their students based on the teachers' presumed superior understanding. When a planner presents the results of many man-years of looking at the environment to a management team, she is usually given the benefit of the doubt: the planner probably knows more about the environment than the management team she is talking to. But when the same planner walks into a boardroom to start teaching about the strategy of the company, her authority disappears. When you cannot be granted authority, you can no longer teach.

FORTIFIED WITH THIS UNDERSTANDING OF planning and its role, we looked for ways to accelerate institutional learning. Curiously enough, we learned in two cases that changing the rules, or suspending them, could be a spur to learning. Rules in a corporation are extremely important. Nobody likes them but everybody obeys them because they are recognized as the glue of the organization. And yet, we have all known extraordinary managers who got their organizations out of a rut by changing the rules. Intuitively they changed the orgnization and the way it looked at matters, and so, as a consequence, accelerated learning.

Several years ago one of our work groups introduced, out of the blue, a new rule into the corporate rain dance: "Thou shalt plan strategically in the first half of the calendar year." (We already had a so-called business planning cycle that dealt with capital budgets in the second half of the calendar year.)

The work group was wise enough not to be too specific about what it had in mind. Some operating companies called up and asked what was meant by "strategic planning." But the answer they got—that ideas were more important than numbers—was vague. Other companies just started to hold strategic planning meetings in the spring.

In the first year the results of this new game were scanty, mostly a rehash of the previous year's business plans. But in the second year the plans were fresher and each year the quality of thinking that went into strategic planning improved. So we asked ourselves whether, by having changed the rules of the game—because that's what the planning system is, one of the rules of the corporate game—we had accelerated institutional learning. And our answer was yes. We changed the rules and the corporation played by the new rules that evolved in the process.

A similar thing happened when we tried suspending
the rules. In 1984 we had a scenario that talked about
$15-a-barrel oil. (Bear in mind that in 1984 the price of a
barrel of oil was $28 and $15 was the end of the world to
oil people.) We thought it important that, as early in
1985 as possible, senior managers throughout Shell start
learning about a world of $15 oil. But the response to
this scenario was essentially, "If you want us to think
about this world, first tell us when the price is going to
fall, how far it will fall, and how long the drop will last."

A deadlock ensued which we broke by writing a case
study with a preface that was really a license to play.
"We don't know the future," it said. "But neither do you.
And though none of us knows whether the price is going
to fall, we can agree that it would be pretty serious if it
did. So we have written a case showing one of many possible ways by which the price of oil could fall." We then
described a case in which the price plummeted at the
end of 1985 and concluded by saying: "And now it is
April 1986 and you are staring at a price of $16 a barrel.
Will you please meet and give your views on these three
questions: What do you think your government will do?
What do you think your competition will do? And what,
if anything, will you do?"

Since at that point the price was still $28 and rising,
the case was only a game. But that game started off
serious work throughout Shell, not on answering the
question "What will happen?" but rather exploring the
question "What will we do if it happens?" The accelera-
tion of the institutional learning process had been set in
motion.

As it turned out, the price of oil was still $27 in early
January of 1986. But on February 1 it was $17 and in

April it was $10. The fact that Shell had already visited the world of $15 oil helped a great deal in that panicky spring of 1986.

By now, we knew we were on to something: games could significantly accelerate institutional learning. That's not so strange when you think of it. Some of the most difficult and complex tasks in our lives were learned by playing: cycling, tennis, playing an instrument. We did it, we experimented, we played. But how were we going to make it OK to play?

Few managers are able to say, "I don't mind a little mistake. Go ahead, experiment," especially with a crisis looming. We didn't feel we could go to executives who run some of the biggest companies in the world and say, "Come on, let's have a little game." And in any case, board meetings have agendas, are fixed to end at a certain time, and require certain action to be taken. Still, within these constraints, we have found ways to learn by playing.

ONE CHARACTERISTIC OF PLAY, as the Tavistock Institute in London has shown, is the presence of a transitional object. For the person playing, the transitional object is a representation of the real world. A child who is playing with a doll learns a great deal about the real world at a very fast pace.

Successful consultants let themselves be treated as transitional objects. The process begins when the consultant says something like this to a management team: "We know from experience that many good strategies are largely implicit. If you let us interview people at various levels in your organization, we'll see whether we can get your strategy out on paper. Then we'll come back and check whether we've understood it."

Some weeks later the consultant goes back to the team and says: "Well, we've looked at your strategy and we've played it through a number of likely possibilities, and here is what we think will be the outcome. Do you like it?" The management team will almost certainly say no. So the consultant will say: "All right, let's see how we can change it. Let's go back to your original model and see what was built in there that produced this result." This process is likely to go through a number of iterations, during which the team's original model will change considerably. Those changes constitute the learning that is taking place among the team's members.

Like consultants, computer models can be used to play back and forth management's view of its market, the environment, or the competition. The starting point, however, must be the mental model that the audience has at the moment. If a planner walks into the room with a model on his computer that he has made up himself, the chances are slim that his audience will recognize this particular microworld. If the target group is a management team, the starting model must be the sum of their individual models. How can this be done?

One way is to involve team members in the development of a new common model and leave their individual models implicit. Alternatively, one can bring the individual models out in the open through interviews and make them explicit. In both approaches, computers can serve as transitional objects in which to store the common models that get built.

To most planners, one all-important aspect of these microworlds is counterintuitive: the probability that they have little relation to the real world. God seems to have told model builders that a model should have predictive qualities and that therefore it should represent the real world. In building microworlds, however, this is totally irrelevant. What we want to capture are the models that exist in the minds of the audience. Almost certainly, these will not represent the real world. None of us has a model that actually captures the real world, because no complex reality can be represented analytically and a model is an analytical way of representing reality. Moreover, for the purpose of learning, it is not the reality that matters but the team's model of reality, which will change as members' understanding of their world improves.

But why go to all this trouble? Why not rely on the natural learning process that occurs whenever a management team meets? For us at Shell, there are three compelling reasons. First, although the models in the human mind are complex, most people can deal with only three or four variables at a time and do so through only one or two time iterations.

Look, for instance, at current discussions about the price of oil. Nine out of ten people draw on a price-elasticity model of the market: the price has come down, therefore demand will go up and supply will eventually fall. Ergo, they will conclude, at some time in the future the price of oil must rise. Now we all know that what goes up must come down. But our minds, in thinking through this complex model, work through too few iterations, and we stop at the point where the price goes up. If we computerize the model of the person who stops thinking at the moment the price rises, however, the model will almost certainly show the price falling after its rise. Yet this knowledge would be counterintuitive to the very person (or persons) who built the model.

The second reason for putting mental models into computers is that in working with dynamic models, people discover that in complex systems (like markets or companies) cause and effect are separated in time and place. To many people such insight is also counter-intuitive. Most of us, particularly if we are engaged in the process of planning, focus on the effect we want to create and then look for the most immediate cause to create that effect. The use of dynamic models helps us discover other trigger points, separated in time and place from the desired effect.

Lastly, by using computer models we learn what constitutes relevant information. For only when we start playing with these microworlds do we find out what information we really need to know.

W HEN PEOPLE PLAY with models this way, they are actually creating a new language among themselves that expresses the knowledge they have acquired. And here we come to the most important aspect of institutional learning, whether it be achieved through teaching or through play as we have defined it: the institutional learning process is a process of language development. As the implicit knowledge of each learner becomes explicit, his or her mental model becomes a building block of the institutional model. How much and how fast this model changes will depend on the culture and structure of the organization. Teams that have to cope with rigid procedures and information systems will learn more slowly than those with flexible, open communication channels. Autocratic institutions will learn faster or not at all—the ability of one or a few leaders being a risky institutional bet.

Human beings aren't the only ones whose learning ability is directly related to their ability to convey information. As a species, birds have great potential to learn, but there are important differences among them. Titmice, for example, move in flocks and mix freely, while robins live in well-defined parts of the garden and for the most part communicate antagonistically across the borders of their territories. Virtually all the titmice in the U.K. quickly learned how to pierce the seals of milk bottles left at doorsteps. But robins as a group will never learn to do this (though individual birds may) because their capacity for institutional learning is low; one bird's knowledge does not spread.[4] The same phenomenon occurs in management teams that work by mandate. The best learning takes place in teams that accept that the whole is larger than the sum of the parts, that there is a good that transcends the individual.

What about managers who find themselves in a robin culture? Clearly, their chances of accelerating institutional learning are reduced. Nevertheless, they can take a significant step toward opening up communication and thus the learning process by keeping one fact in mind: institutional learning begins with the calibration of existing mental models.

We are continuing to explore other ways to improve and speed up our institutional learning process. Our exploration into learning through play via a transitional object (a consultant or a computer) looks promising enough at this point to push on in that direction. And while we are navigating in poorly charted waters, we are not out there alone.[5]

Our exploration into this area is not a luxury. We understand that the only competitive advantage the company of the future will have is its managers' ability to learn faster than their competitors. So the companies that succeed will be those that continually nudge their managers towards revising their views of the world. The challenges for the planner are considerable. So are the rewards.

# Notes

1. I use the collective expression "Shell" for convenience when referring to the companies of the Royal Dutch/Shell Group in general, or when no purpose is served by identifying the particular Shell company or companies.

2. Pierre Wack wrote about our system in "Scenarios: Uncharted Waters Ahead," HBR September–October 1985, p. 72 and in "Scenarios: Shooting the Rapids," HBR November–December 1985, p. 139.

3. John Holt, *How Children Learn,* rev. ed. (New York: Delacorte, 1983) and John Holt, *How Children Fail,* rev. ed. (New York: Delacorte, 1982).

4. Jeff S. Wyles, Joseph G. Kunkel, and Allan C. Wilson, "Birds, Behavior and Anatomical Evolution," *Proceedings of the National Academy of Sciences,* USA, July 1983.

5. Through MIT's Program in Systems Thinking and the New Management Style, a group of senior executives are looking at this and other issues.

Originally published in March–April 1988
Reprint 88202

# The Right Game

## Use Game Theory to Shape Strategy

ADAM M. BRANDENBURGER AND

BARRY J. NALEBUFF

## Executive Summary

BUSINESS IS A HIGH-STAKES GAME. The way we approach this game is reflected in the language we use to describe it. Business language is full of expressions borrowed from the military and from sports. Unlike war and sports, however, business is not about winning and losing. Companies can succeed without requiring others to fail. And they can fail no matter how well they play if they play the wrong game.

The essence of business success lies in making sure you're playing the right game. How do you know if it's the right game? What can you do if it's the wrong game? To help managers answer those questions, the authors have developed a framework that draws on the insights of game theory.

The primary insight of game theory is the importance of focusing on others—of putting yourself in the shoes of other players and trying to play out all the reactions to their actions as far ahead as possible. By adopting this perspective, a company may, for example, discover that its chances for success are greater if it creates a win-win, rather than a win-lose, situation with other players. In other words, companies should consider both cooperative and competitive ways to change the game.

Who are the participants in the game of business? The authors introduce a schematic map that represents all the players and all the interdependencies among them. Drawing this map for your business is the first step toward changing the game. The second step is identifying all five elements of the game—players, added values, rules, tactics, and scope—and changing one or more of them. By using these tools, the authors say, companies can design a game that's right for them.

---

Business is a high-stakes game. The way we approach this game is reflected in the language we use to describe it. Business language is full of expressions borrowed from the military and from sports. Some of them are dangerously misleading. Unlike war and sports, business is not about winning and losing. Nor is it about how well you play the game. Companies can succeed spectacularly without requiring others to fail. And they can fail miserably no matter how well they play if they make the mistake of playing the wrong game.

The essence of business success lies in making sure you're playing the right game. How do you know if it's the right game? What can you do about it if it's the wrong game? To help managers answer those questions, we've developed a framework that draws on the insights of game theory. After 50 years as a mathematical construct, game theory is about to change the game of business.

Game theory came of age in 1994, when three pioneers in the field were awarded the Nobel Prize. It all began in 1944, when mathematics genius John von Neumann and economist Oskar Morgenstern published their book *Theory of Games and Economic Behavior.* Immediately heralded as one of the greatest scientific achievements of the century, their work provided a systematic way to understand the behavior of players in situations where their fortunes are interdependent. Von Neumann and Morgenstern distinguished two types of games. In the first type, rule-based games, players interact according to specified "rules of engagement." These rules might come from contracts, loan covenants, or trade agreements, for example. In the second type, freewheeling games, players interact without any external constraints. For example, buyers and sellers may create value by transacting in an unstructured fashion. Business is a complex mix of both types of games.

For rule-based games, game theory offers the principle, To every action, there is a reaction. But, unlike Newton's third law of motion, the reaction is not programmed to be equal and opposite. To analyze how other players will react to your move, you need to play out all the reactions (including yours) to their actions as far ahead as possible. You have to look forward far into the game and then reason backward to figure out which of today's actions will lead you to where you want to end up.[1]

For freewheeling games, game theory offers the principle, You cannot take away from the game more than you bring to it. In business, what does a particular player bring to the game? To find the answer, look at the value created when everyone is in the game, and then pluck that player out and see how much value the remaining players can create. The difference is the removed player's "added value." In unstructured interactions, you cannot take away more than your added value.[2]

Underlying both principles is a shift in perspective. Many people view games egocentrically—that is, they focus on their own position. The primary insight of game theory is the importance of focusing on others—namely, allocentrism. To look forward and reason backward, you have to put

*Successful business strategy is about actively shaping the game you play, not just playing the game you find.*

yourself in the shoes–even in the heads–of other players. To assess your added value, you have to ask not what other players can bring to you but what you can bring to other players.

Managers can profit by using these insights from game theory to design a game that is right for their companies. The rewards that can come from changing a game may be far greater than those from maintaining the status quo. For example, Nintendo succeeded brilliantly in changing the video game business by taking control of software. Sega's subsequent success required changing the game again. Rupert Murdoch's *New York Post* changed the tabloid game by finding a convincing way to demonstrate the cost of a price war without actually launching one. BellSouth made money by changing the takeover game between Craig McCaw and Lin Broadcasting. Successful business strategy is about actively shaping the game you play, not just playing the game you find. We will explore how these examples and others worked in practice, starting with the story of how General Motors changed the game of selling cars.

## From Lose-Lose to Win-Win

In the early 1990s, the U.S. automobile industry was locked into an all-too-familiar mode of destructive competition. End-of-year rebates and dealer discounts were ruining the industry's profitability. As soon as one company used incentives to clear excess inventory at year-end, others had to do the same. Worse still, consumers came to expect the rebates. As a result, they waited for them to be offered before buying a car, forcing manufacturers to offer incentives earlier in the year. Was there a way out? Would someone find an alternative to practices that were hurting all the companies? General Motors may have done just that.

In September 1992, General Motors and Household Bank issued a new credit card that allowed cardholders to apply 5% of their charges toward buying or leasing a new GM car, up to $500 per year, with a maximum of $3,500. The GM card has been the most successful credit-card launch in history. One month after it was introduced, there were 1.2 million accounts. Two years later, there were 8.7 million accounts—and the program is still growing. Projections suggest that eventually some 30% of GM's nonfleet sales in North America will be to cardholders.

As Hank Weed, managing director of GM's card program, explains, the card helps GM build share through the "conquest" of prospective Ford buyers and others—a traditional win-lose strategy. But the program has engineered another, more subtle change in the game of selling cars. It replaced other incentives that GM had previously offered. The net effect has been to raise the price that a noncard-holder—someone who intends to buy a Ford, for example—would have to pay for a GM car. The program thus gives Ford some breathing room to raise its prices. That allows GM, in turn, to raise its prices without losing customers to Ford. The result is a win-win dynamic between GM and Ford.

If the GM card is as good as it sounds, what's stopping other companies from copying it? Not much, it seems. First, Ford introduced its version of the program with Citibank. Then Volkswagen introduced its variation with MBNA Corporation. Doesn't all this imitation put a dent in the GM program? Not necessarily.

Imitation is the sincerest form of flattery, but in business it is often thought to be a killer compliment. Textbooks on strategy warn that if others can imitate something you do, you can't make money at it. Some go even further, asserting that business strategy cannot be codified. If it could, it would be imitated and any gains would evaporate.

Yet the proponents of this belief are mistaken in assuming that imitation is always harmful. It's true that once GM's program is widely imitated, the company's ability to lure customers away from other manufacturers will be diminished. But imitation also can help GM. Ford and Volkswagen offset the cost of their credit card rebates by scaling back other incentive programs. The result was an effective price increase for GM customers, the vast majority of whom do not participate in the Ford and Volkswagen credit card programs. This gives GM the option to firm up its demand or raise its prices further. All three car companies now have a more loyal customer base, so there is less incentive to compete on price.

To understand the full impact of the GM card program, you have to use game theory. You can't see all the ramifications of the program without adopting an allocentric perspective. The key is to anticipate how Ford, Volkswagen, and other automakers will respond to GM's initiative.

When you change the game, you want to come out ahead. That's pretty clear. But what about the fact that GM's strategy helped Ford? One common mind-set—seeing business as war—says that others have to lose in order for you to win. There may indeed be times when you want to opt for a win-lose strategy. But not always. The GM example shows that there also are times when you want to create a win-win situation. Although it may sound surprising, sometimes the best way to succeed is to let others, including your competitors, do well.

Looking for win-win strategies has several advantages. First, because the approach is relatively unexplored, there is greater potential for finding new opportunities. Second, because others are not being forced to give up ground, they may offer less resistance to win-win moves, making them easier to implement. Third, because win-win moves don't force other players to retaliate, the new game is more sustainable. And finally, imitation of a win-win move is beneficial, not harmful.

To encourage thinking about both cooperative and competitive ways to change the game, we suggest the term *coopetition.*[3] It means looking for win-win as well as win-lose opportunities. Keeping both possibilities in mind is important because win-lose strategies often backfire. Consider, for example, the common—and dangerous—strategy of lowering prices to gain market share. Although it may provide a temporary benefit, the gains will evaporate if others match the cuts to regain their lost share. The result is simply to reestablish the status quo but at lower prices—a lose-lose scenario that leaves all the players worse off. That was the situation in the automobile industry before GM changed the game.

## The Game of Business

Did GM intentionally plan to change the game of selling cars in the way we have described it? Or did the company just get lucky with a loyalty marketing program that turned out better than anyone had expected? Looking back, the one thing we can say with certainty is that the stakes in situations like GM's are too high to be left to chance. That's why we have developed a comprehensive map and a method to help managers find strategies for changing the game.

The game of business is all about value: creating it and capturing it. Who are the participants in this enterprise? To describe them, we introduce the Value Net—a schematic map designed to represent all the players in the game and the interdependencies among them. (See the exhibit "Who Are the Players in Your Company's Value Net?")

Interactions take place along two dimensions. Along the vertical dimension are the company's customers and suppliers. Resources such as labor and raw materials flow from the suppliers to the company, and products and services flow from the company to its customers. Money flows in the reverse direction, from customers to the company and from the company to its suppliers. Along the horizontal dimension are the players with whom the company interacts but does not transact. They are its *substitutors* and *complementors*.

Substitutors are alternative players from whom customers may purchase products or to whom suppliers may sell their resources. Coca-Cola and Pepsico are substitutors with respect to consumers because they sell rival colas. A little less obvious is that Coca-Cola and Tyson Foods are substitutors with respect to suppliers. That is because both companies use carbon dioxide. Tyson uses it for freezing chickens, and Coke uses it for carbonation. (As they say in the cola industry, "No fizziness, no bizziness.")

Complementors are players from whom customers buy complementary products or to whom suppliers sell complementary resources. For example, hardware and software companies are classic complementors. Faster hardware, such as a Pentium chip, increases users' willingness to pay for more powerful software. More powerful software, such as the latest version of Microsoft Office, increases users' willingness to pay for faster hardware. American Airlines and United Air Lines, though substitutors with respect to passengers, are complementors when they decide to update their fleets. That's because Boeing can recoup the cost of a new plane design only if enough airlines buy it. Since each airline

**Who Are the Players in Your Company's Value Net?**

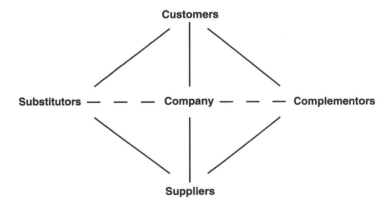

effectively subsidizes the other's purchase of planes, the two are complementors in this instance.

We introduce the terms *substitutor* and *complementor* because we find that the traditional business vocabulary inhibits a full understanding of the interdependencies that exist in business. If you call a player a competitor, you tend to focus on competing rather than on finding opportunities for cooperation. *Substitutor* describes the market relationship without that prejudice. Complementors, often overlooked in traditional strategic analysis, are the natural counterparts of substitutors.

The Value Net describes the various roles of the players. It's possible for the same player to occupy more than one role simultaneously. Remember that American and United are both substitutors and complementors. Gary Hamel and C.K. Prahalad make this point in *Competing for the Future* (Harvard Business School Press, 1994): "On any given day . . . AT&T might find Motorola to be a supplier, a buyer, a competitor, *and* a partner."

The Value Net reveals two fundamental symmetries in the game of business: the first between customers and suppliers and the second between substitutors and complementors. Understanding those symmetries can help managers come up with new strategies for changing the game or new applications of existing strategies.

Managers understand intuitively that along the vertical dimension of the Value Net, there is a mixture of cooperation and competition. It's cooperation when suppliers, companies, and customers come together to create value in the first place. It's competition when the time comes for them to divide the pie.

Along the horizontal dimension, however, managers tend to see only half the picture. Substitutors are seen only as enemies. Complementors, if viewed at all, are seen only as friends. Such a perspective overlooks another symmetry. There can be a cooperative element to interactions with substitutors, as the GM story illustrates, and a competitive element to interactions with complementors, as we will see.

## Changing the Game

The Value Net is a map that prompts you to explore all the interdependencies in the game. Drawing the Value Net for your business is therefore the first step toward changing the game. The second step is identifying all the elements of the game. According to game theory, there are five: players, added values, rules, tactics, and scope—PARTS for short. These five elements fully describe all interactions, both freewheeling and rule-based. To change the game, you have to change one or more of these elements.

*None of the players are fixed. Sometimes it's smart to change who is playing the game. That includes yourself.*

*Players* come first. As we saw in the Value Net, the players are customers, suppliers, substitutors, and complementors. None of the players are fixed. Sometimes it's smart to change who is playing the game. That includes yourself.

*Added values* are what each player brings to the game. There are ways to make yourself a more valuable player—in other words, to raise your added value. And there are ways to lower the added values of other players.

*Rules* give structure to the game. In business, there is no universal set of rules; a rule might arise from law, custom, practicality, or contracts. In addition to using existing rules to their advantage, players may be able to revise them or come up with new ones.

*Tactics* are moves used to shape the way players perceive the game and hence how they play. Sometimes, tactics are designed to reduce misperceptions; at other times, they are designed to create or maintain uncertainty.

*Scope* describes the boundaries of the game. It's possible for players to expand or shrink those boundaries.

Successful business strategies begin by assessing and then changing one or more of these elements. PARTS does more than exhort you to think out of the box. It provides the tools to enable you to do so. Let's look at each strategic lever in turn.

## Changing the Players

NutraSweet, a low-calorie sweetener used in soft drinks such as Diet Coke and Diet Pepsi, is a household name, and its swirl logo is recognized world-wide. In fact, it's Monsanto's brand name for the chemical aspartame. NutraSweet has been a very profitable business for Monsanto, with 70% gross margins. Such profits usually attract others to enter the market, but NutraSweet was protected by patents in Europe until 1987 and in the United States until 1992.

With Coke's blessing, a challenger, the Holland Sweetener Company, built an aspartame plant in Europe in 1985 in anticipation of the patent expiration. Ken Dooley, HSC's vice president of marketing and sales, explained, "Every manufacturer likes to have at least two sources of supply."

As HSC attacked the European market, Monsanto fought back aggressively. It used deep price cuts and contractual relationships with customers to deny HSC a toehold in the market. HSC managed to fend off the initial counterattack by appealing to the courts to enable it to gain access to customers. Dooley considered all this just a preview of things to come: "We are looking forward to moving the war into the United States."

But Dooley's war ended before it began. Just prior to the U.S. patent expiration, both Coke and Pepsi signed new long-term contracts with Monsanto. When at last there was a real potential for competition between suppliers, it appeared that Coke and Pepsi didn't seize the opportunity. Or did they?

Neither Coke nor Pepsi ever had any real desire to switch over to generic aspartame. Remembering the result of the New Coke reformulation of 1985, neither company wanted to be the first to take the NutraSweet logo off the can and create a perception that it was fooling around with the flavor of its drinks. If only one switched over, the other most certainly would

*Neither Coke nor Pepsi wanted to be the first to take the NutraSweet logo off the can and create a perception that it was fooling around with the flavor of its drinks.*

have made a selling point of its exclusive use of NutraSweet. After all, NutraSweet had already built a reputation for safety and good taste. Even though generic aspartame would taste the same, consumers would be unfamiliar with the unbranded product and see it as inferior. Another reason not to switch was that Monsanto had spent the previous decade marching down the learning curve for making aspartame–giving it a significant cost advantage—while HSC was still near the top.

In the end, what Coke and Pepsi really wanted was to get the same old NutraSweet at a much better price. That they accomplished. Look at Monsanto's position before and after HSC entered the game. Before, there was no good substitute for NutraSweet. Cyclamates had been banned, and saccharin caused cancer in laboratory rats. NutraSweet's added value was its ability to make a safe, good-tasting low-calorie drink possible. Stir in a patent and things looked very positive for Monsanto. When HSC came along, NutraSweet's added value was greatly reduced. What was left was its brand loyalty and its manufacturing cost advantage.

Where did all this leave HSC? Clearly, its entry into the market was worth a lot to Coke and Pepsi. It would have been quite reasonable for HSC, before entering the market, to demand compensation for its role in the form of either a fixed payment or a guaranteed contract. But, once in, with an unbranded product and higher production costs, it was much more difficult for the company to make money. Dooley was right when he said that all manufacturers want a second source. The problem is, they don't necessarily want to do much business with that source.

Monsanto did well to create a brand identity and a cost advantage: It minimized the negative effects of entry by a generic brand. Coke and Pepsi did well to change the game by encouraging the entry of a new player that would reduce their dependence on NutraSweet. According to HSC, the new contracts led to combined savings of $200 million annually for Coke and Pepsi. As for HSC, perhaps it was too quick to become a player. The question for HSC was not what it could do for Coke and Pepsi; the question was what Coke and Pepsi could do for HSC. Although it was a duopolist in a weak position when it came to selling aspartame, HSC was a monopolist in a strong position when it came to selling its "service" to make the aspartame market competitive. Perhaps Coke and Pepsi would have paid a higher price for this valuable service, but only if HSC had demanded such payment up front.

## PAY ME TO PLAY

As the NutraSweet story illustrates, sometimes the most valuable service you can offer is creating competition, so don't give it away for free. People in the takeover game have long understood the art of getting paid to play. The cellular phone business was undergoing rapid consolidation in June 1989, when 39-year-old Craig McCaw made a bid for Lin Broadcasting Corporation. With 50 million POPs (lingo for the population in a coverage area) already under his belt, McCaw saw the acquisition of Lin's 18 million POPs as the best, and possibly the only, way to acquire a national cellular footprint. He bid $120 per share for Lin, which resulted in an immediate jump in Lin's share price from $103.50 to $129.50. Clearly, the market expected more action. But Lin's CEO, Donald Pels, didn't care much for McCaw or his bid. Faced with Lin's hostile reaction, McCaw lowered his offer to $110, and Lin sought other suitors. BellSouth, with 28 million POPs, was the natural alternative, although acquiring Lin wouldn't quite give it a national footprint.

Nevertheless, BellSouth was willing to acquire Lin for the right price. But if it entered the fray, it would create a bidding war and thus make it unlikely that Lin would be sold for a reasonable price. BellSouth knew that only one bidder could win, and it wanted something in case that bidder was McCaw. Thus, as a condition for making

a bid, BellSouth got Lin's promise of a $54 million conso-
lation prize and an additional $15 million toward
expenses in the event that it was outbid. BellSouth made
an offer generally valued at between $105 and $112 per
share. As expected, BellSouth was outbid; McCaw
responded with an offer
valued at $112 to $118
per share. BellSouth
then raised its bid to
roughly $120 per share.
In return, Lin raised
BellSouth's expense cap
to $25 million. McCaw raised his bid to $130 and then
added a few dollars more to close the deal. At the same
time, he paid BellSouth $22.5 million to exit the game.[4]
At this point in the bidding, Lin's CEO recognized that
his stock options were worth $186 million, and the now
friendly deal with McCaw was concluded.

*BellSouth understood that
even if you can't make
money in the game the old-
fashioned way, you can
get paid to change it.*

So how did the various players make out? Lin got
itself an extra billion, which made its $79 million pay-
ment to BellSouth look like a bargain. McCaw got the
national network he wanted and subsequently sold out
to AT&T, making himself a billionaire. And BellSouth,
by getting paid first to play and then to go away, turned
a weak hand into $76.5 million plus expenses.

BellSouth clearly understood that even if you can't
make money in the game the old-fashioned way, you can
get paid to change it. Such payments need not be made
in cash; you can ask for a guaranteed sales contract, contributions to R&D, bid-preparation expenses, or a last-
look provision.

The examples so far show how you can change three
of the four players in the Value Net. Lin paid to bring in
an extra buyer, or customer. Coke and Pepsi would, no

doubt, have been prepared to pay HSC handsomely to become a second supplier. And McCaw paid to take out a rival bidder, or substitutor. That leaves complementors. The next example shows how a company can benefit from bringing players into the complements market.

## CHEAP COMPLEMENTS

Remember that hardware is the classic complement to software. One can't function without the other. Software writers won't produce programs unless a sufficient hardware base exists. Yet consumers won't purchase the hardware until a critical mass of software exists. 3DO Company, a maker of video games, is attacking this chicken-and-egg problem in the video-game business by bringing players into the complements market. To those who know 3DO's founder, Trip Hawkins, this should come as no surprise: He designed his own major at Harvard in strategy and game theory.

3DO owns a 32-bit CD-ROM hardware-and-software technology for next-generation video games. The company plans to make money by licensing software houses to make 3DO games and collecting a $3 royalty fee (hence the company name). Of course, to sell software, you first need people to buy the hardware. But those early adopters won't find much software. To start the ball rolling, 3DO needs the hardware to be cheap—the cheaper the better.

The company's strategy is to give away the license to produce the hardware technology. This move has induced hardware manufacturers such as Panasonic (Matsushita), GoldStar, Sanyo, and Toshiba to enter the game. Because all 3DO software will run on all 3DO hardware, the hardware manufacturers are left to compete on cost alone. Making the hardware a commodity is just what 3DO wants: It drives down the price of the complementary product.

But not quite enough. 3DO is discovering that to create momentum in the market, the hardware must be sold below cost, and hardware manufacturers aren't willing to go that far. As an inducement, 3DO now offers them two shares of 3DO stock for each machine sold. The company also has renegotiated its deal with software houses up to a $6 royalty, with the extra $3 earmarked to subsidize hardware sales. So Hawkins is actually paying people to play in the complements market. Is he paying enough? Time will tell.

Creating competition in the complements market is the flip side of coopetition. Just as substitutors are usually seen only as enemies, complementors are seen only as friends. Whereas the GM story shows the possibility of win-win opportunities with substitutors, the 3DO example illustrates the possibility of legitimate win-lose opportunities with complementors. Creating competition among its complementors helped 3DO at their expense.

## Changing the Added Values

Just as you shouldn't accept the players of a game as fixed, you shouldn't take what they bring to the game as fixed, either. You can change the players' added values. Common sense tells us that there are two options: Raise your own added value or lower that of others.

Good basic business practices are one route to raising added values. You can tailor your product to customers' needs, build a brand, use resources more efficiently, work with your suppliers to lower their costs, and so on.

These strategies should not be underestimated. But there are other, less transparent ways to raise your added value. As an example, consider Trans World Airlines' introduction of Comfort Class in 1993.

Robert Cozzi, TWA's senior vice president of marketing, proposed removing 5 to 40 seats per plane to give passengers in coach more legroom. The move raised TWA's added value; according to J.D. Power and Associates, the company soared to first place in customer satisfaction for long-haul flights

*After TWA removed seats to create more legroom in coach, its renamed Comfort Class placed first in customer satisfaction.*

This was a win for TWA and a loss for other airlines. But elements of win-win were present as well: With fuller planes, TWA was not about to start a price war.

But what if other carriers copied the strategy? Would that negate TWA's efforts? No, because as others copied TWA's move, excess capacity would be retired from an industry plagued by overcapacity. Passengers get more legroom, and carriers stop flying empty seats around. Everyone wins. Cozzi saw a way to move the industry away from the self-defeating price competition that goes on when airlines try to fill up the coach cabin. This was business strategy at its best.[5]

The idea of raising your own added value is natural. Less intuitive is the approach of lowering the added value of others. To illustrate how the strategy works, let's begin with a simple card game.

Adam and 26 of his M.B.A. students are playing a card game. Adam has 26 black cards, and each of the students has one red card. Any red card coupled with a black card gets a $100 prize (paid by the dean). How do we expect the bargaining between Adam and his students to proceed?

First, calculate the added values. Without Adam and his black cards, there is no game. Thus Adam's added value equals the total value of the game, which is $2,600. Each student has an added value of $100 because without that student's card, one less match can be made and thus $100 is lost. The sum of the added values is therefore $5,200—made up of $2,600 from Adam and $100 from each of the 26 students. Alas, there is only $2,600 to be divided. Given the symmetry of the game, it's most likely that everyone will end up with half of his or her added value: Adam will buy the students' cards for $50 each or sell his for $50 each.

*The idea of raising your own added value is natural. Less intuitive is the approach of lowering the added value of others.*

So far, nothing is surprising. Could Adam do any better? Yes, but first he'd have to change the game. In a public display, Adam burns three of his black cards. True, the pie is now smaller, at $2,300, and so is Adam's added value. But the point of this strategic move is to destroy the added values of the other players. Now no student has any added value because 3 students are going to end up without a match, and therefore no one student is essential to the game. The total value with 26 students is $2,300, and the total value with 25 students is still $2,300.

At this point, the division will not be equal. Indeed, because no student has any added value, Adam would be quite generous to offer a 90:10 split. Since 3 students will end up with nothing, anyone who ends up with $10 should consider himself or herself lucky. For Adam, 90%

of \$2,300 is a lot better than half of \$2,600. Of course, his getting it depends on the students' not being able to get together; if they did, that would be changing the game, too. In fact, it would be changing the players, as in the previous section, and it would be an excellent strategy for the students to adopt.

Just a card trick? No—a strategy employed by the videogame maker Nintendo (which, it so happens, used to produce playing cards). To see how the company lowered everyone else's added value, we take a tour around its Value Net. (See the exhibit "Nintendo Trumped Every Player in Its Value Net.")

## NINTENDO POWER

Start with Nintendo's customers. Nintendo sold its games to a highly concentrated market—predominantly megaretailers such as Toys "R" Us and Wal-Mart. How

**Nintendo Trumped Every Player in its Value Net**

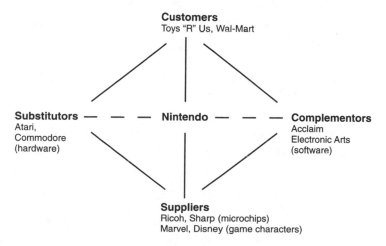

could Nintendo combat such buyer power? By changing the game. Nintendo did just what Adam did when he burned the cards (although Nintendo made a lot more money): It didn't fill all the retailers' orders. In 1988, Nintendo sold 33 million cartridges, but the market could have absorbed 45 million. Poor planning? No. It's true that the pie shrank a little as some stores sold out of the game. But the important point is that retailers lost added value. Even a giant like Toys "R" Us was in a weaker position when not every retailer could get supplied. As Nintendo-mania took hold, consumers queued up outside stores and retailers clamored for more of the product. With games in short supply, Nintendo had zapped the buyers' power.

The next arena of negotiations concerned the complementors—namely, outside game developers. What was Nintendo's strategy? First, it developed software in-house. The company built a security chip into the hardware and then instituted a licensing program for outside developers. The number of licenses was restricted, and licensees were allowed to develop only a limited number of games. Because there were many Nintendo wanna-be programmers and because the company could develop games in-house, the added value of those that did get the license was lowered. Once again, Nintendo ensured that there were fewer black cards than red. It held all the bargaining chips.

Nintendo's suppliers, too, had little added value. The company used old-generation chip technology, making its chips something of a commodity. Another input was the leading characters in the games. Nintendo hit the jackpot by developing Mario. After he became a hit in his own right, the added value of comic-book heroes licensed from others, such as Spiderman (Marvel), and of cartoon icons, such as Mickey Mouse (Disney), was reduced. In fact, Nintendo turned the tables completely, licensing Mario to appear in comic books and on cartoon shows, cereal boxes, board games, and toys.

Finally, there were Nintendo's substitutors. From a kid's perspective, there were no good alternatives to a video game; the only real threat came from alternative video-game systems. Here Nintendo had the game practically all to itself. Having the largest installed base of systems allowed the company to drive down the manufacturing cost for its hardware. And with developers keen to write for the largest installed base, Nintendo got the best games. This created a positive feedback loop: More people bought Nintendo's systems, leading to a larger base, still lower costs, and even more games. Nintendo locked in its lead by requiring exclusivity from outside game developers. With few alternatives to Nintendo, that was a small price for them to pay. Potential challengers couldn't simply take successful games over to their platforms; they had to start from scratch. Although large profits might normally invite entry, no challenger could engineer any added value. The installed base, combined with Nintendo's exclusivity agreements, made competing in Nintendo's game hopeless.

What was the bottom line for Nintendo? How much could a manufacturer of a two-bit—well, eight-bit—game about a lugubrious plumber called Mario really be worth? How about more than Sony or Nissan? Between July 1990 and June 1991, Nintendo's average market value was 2.4 trillion yen, Sony's was 2.2 trillion yen, and Nissan's was 2 trillion yen.

The Nintendo example illustrates the importance of added value as opposed to value. There is no doubt that cars, televisions, and VCRs create more value in the world than do Game Boys. But it's not enough simply to create value; profits come from capturing value. By keeping its added value high and everyone else's low, Nintendo was able to capture a giant slice of a largish pie. The name of the enthusiasts' monthly magazine, *Nintendo Power,* summed up the situation quite nicely.

Nintendo's success, however, brought it under scrutiny. In late 1989, Congressman Dennis Eckart (D-Ohio), chairman of the House Subcommittee on Antitrust, Impact of Deregulation and Privatization, requested that the U.S. Justice Department investigate allegations that Nintendo of America unfairly reduced competition. Eckart's letter argued, among other things, that the Christmas shortages in 1988 were "contrived to increase consumer prices and demand and to enhance Nintendo's market leverage" and that software producers had "become almost entirely dependent on Nintendo's acceptance of their games." None of Nintendo's practices were found to be illegal.[6]

## PUMPING UP PROFITS

Protecting your added value is as important as establishing it in the first place. Back in the mid-1970s, Robert Taylor, CEO of Minnetonka, had the idea for Softsoap, a liquid soap that would be dispensed by a pump. The problem was that it would be hard to retain any added value once the likes of Procter & Gamble and Lever Brothers muscled in with their brands and distribution clout. Nothing in the product could be patented. But, to his credit, Taylor realized that the hardest part of producing the soap was manufacturing the little plastic pump, for which there were just two suppliers. In a bet-the-company move, he locked up both suppliers' total annual production by ordering 100 million of the pumps.

Even at 12 cents apiece, this was a $12 million order— more than Minnetonka's net worth. Ultimately, the major players did enter the market, but capturing the supply of pumps gave Taylor a head start of 12 to 18 months. That advantage preserved Softsoap's added value during this period, allowing the company to build brand loyalty, which continues to provide added value to . this day.

As the TWA, Nintendo, and Softsoap examples illustrate, added values can be changed. By reengineering them—raising your added value and lowering others'— you may be able to capture a larger slice of pie.

Game theory holds that in freewheeling interactions, no player can take away more than that player brings to the game, but that's not quite the end of the matter. First, there is no guarantee that any player will get all its added value. Typically, the sum of all the added values exceeds the total value of the game. Remember that in Adam's card game, the total prize was only $2,600 even though the added values of all the players initially totaled $5,200. Second, even if you have no added value, that doesn't prohibit you from making money. Others might be willing to pay you to enter or exit the game (as with BellSouth); similarly, you might be paid to stay out or stay in. Third, rules constrain interactions among players. We will see that in games with rules, some players may be able to capture more than their added values.

## Changing the Rules

Rules determine how the game is played by limiting the possible reactions to any action. To analyze the effect of a rule, you have to look forward and reason backward.

The simplest rule is *one price to all*. According to this rule, prices are not negotiated individually with each customer. Consequently, a company can profitably enter a market even when it has no added value. If a new player enters with a price lower than the incumbent's, the incumbent has only two effective responses: match the newcomer's price across the board or stand pat and give up share. By looking forward and reasoning backward, a small newcomer can steer the incumbent toward accommodation rather than retaliation.

Imagine that a new player comes in with a limited capacity—say, 10% of the market—and a discounted price. Whether it makes any money depends on how the incumbent responds. The incumbent can recapture its lost market by coming down to match the newcomer's price, or it can give up 10% share. For the incumbent, giving up 10% share is usually better than sacrificing its profit margin. In such cases, the newcomer will do all right. But it can't get too greedy. If it tries to take away too much of the market, the incumbent will choose to give up its profit margin in order to regain share. Only when the newcomer limits its capacity does the incumbent stand pat and the newcomer make money. For this reason, the strategy is called *judo economics:* By staying small, the newcomer turns the incumbent's larger size to its own benefit.

To pull off a judo strategy, the newcomer's commitment to limit its capacity must be both clear and credible. The newcomer may be tempted to expand, but it must realize that if it does, it will give the incumbent an incentive to retaliate.

## KIWI IS NO DODO

Kiwi International Air Lines understands these ideas perfectly. Named for the flightless bird, Kiwi is a 1992 start-up founded by former Eastern Air Lines pilots who were grounded after Eastern went bankrupt. Kiwi engineered a cost advantage from its employee ownership and its use of leased planes. But it had lower name recognition and a more limited flight schedule than the major carriers—on balance, not much, if any, added value. So what did it do? It went for low prices and limited capacity. According to public statements from its then CEO, Robert Iverson, "We designed our system to stay out of the way of large carriers and to make sure they understand that we pose no threat. . . . Kiwi intends to capture, at most, only 10% share of any one market—or no more than four flights per day." Because Kiwi targets business travelers, the major airlines can't use stay-over and advance-purchase restrictions to lower price selectively against it. So Kiwi benefited from the one-price-to-all rule.

Now Kiwi, in turn, became the large player for any newcomer to the same market. That didn't leave much room to be small in relation to Kiwi, so Kiwi had to fight if someone else tried to follow suit. According to Iverson, "[The major airlines] are better off with us than without us." Even though Kiwi was Delta's rival, by staying small and keeping out other potential entrants, it managed to bring an element of coopetition into the game. From Delta's perspective, Kiwi was rather like the devil it knew.

The Kiwi story illustrates how a player can take advantage of existing rules of the marketplace—in this case, the one-price-to-all rule. In addition to practicality, rules arise from custom, law, or contracts. Common contract-based rules are most-favored-nation (most-favored-customer) clauses, take-or-pay agreements, and meet-the-competition clauses. These rules give structure to negotiations between buyers and sellers. Rules are particularly useful for players in commodity-like businesses. As an example, take the carbon dioxide industry.

## SOLID PROFITS FROM GAS

There are three major producers of carbon dioxide: Airco, Liquid Carbonic, and Air Liquide. Carbon dioxide creates enormous value (in carbonation and freezing), but it is essentially a commodity, which makes it hard for a producer to capture any of that value. One distinguishing factor, however, is that carbon dioxide is very expensive to transport, which gives some added value to the producer best located to serve a specific customer. Other sources of added value are differentiation through reliability, reputation, service, and technology. Still, a producer's added value is usually small in relation to the total value created. The question is, Can a producer capture more than its added value?

In this case the answer is yes, because of the rules of the game in the carbon dioxide industry. The producers have a meet-the-competition clause (MCC) in their contracts with customers. An MCC gives the incumbent seller the right to make the last bid.

The result of an MCC is that a producer can sustain a higher price and thereby earn more than its added value. Normally, an elevated price would invite other producers to compete on price. In this case, however, a challenger cannot come in and take away business simply by undercutting the existing price. If it tried, the

*Can a producer capture more than its added value? With the carbon dioxide industry's meet-the-competition clause, it can.*

incumbent could then come back with a lower price and keep the business. The back-and-forth could go on until the price fell to variable cost, but at that point stealing the business wouldn't be worth the effort. The only one to benefit would be the buyer, who would end up with a lower price.

Cutting price to go after an incumbent's business is always risky but may be justified by the gain in business. Not so when the incumbent has an MCC: The upside is lost and the downside remains. Lowering price sets a dangerous precedent and increases the likelihood of a tit-for-tat response. The incumbent may retaliate by going after the challenger's business, and even if the challenger doesn't lose customers, it certainly will lose profits. Another downside is that the challenger's customers may end up at a disadvantage. If the challenger supplies Coke and the incumbent supplies Pepsi, the challenger shouldn't help Pepsi get a lower price. Its future is tied to Coke, and it doesn't want to give Pepsi any cost advantage. It might even end up having to lower its own price to Coke without getting Pepsi's business. Finally, the challenger's efforts are misplaced: It would do better to make sure that its existing customers are happy.

Putting in an MCC changes the game in a way that's clearly a win for the incumbent. Perhaps surprisingly, the challenger also ends up better off. True, it may not be able to take away market share, but the incumbent's higher prices set a good precedent: They give the challenger some room to raise prices to its own customers. There also is less danger that the incumbent will go after the challenger's share, because the incumbent, with higher profits, now has more to lose. An MCC is a classic case of coopetition.

As for the customers, why do they go along with this rule? It may be traditional in their industry. Perhaps it's the norm. Perhaps they decide to trade an initial price break in return for the subsequent lock-in. Or maybe they don't thoroughly understand the rule's implications. Whatever the reason, MCCs do offer benefits to customers. The clauses guarantee producers a long-term relationship if they so choose, even in the absence of long-term contracts. Thus producers are more willing to invest in serving their customers. Finally, even if there is no formal MCC, it's generally accepted that you don't leave your current supplier without giving it a last chance to bid.

Using an MCC is a strategy that, far from being undermined by imitation, is enhanced by it. A carbon dioxide producer benefits from unilateral adoption of an MCC, but there is an added kicker when other producers copy it. The MCCs allow them to push prices up further, so they now have even more to lose from starting a share war. As MCCs become more widespread, everyone has less prospect of

*If negotiations in your business take place without rules, consider how bringing in a new rule would change the game. But be careful.*

gaining share. With even more at risk and even less to gain, producers refrain from going after one another's customers. A moral: Players who live in glass houses are unlikely to throw stones. So you should be pleased when others build glass houses.

Both the significance of rules and the opportunity to change the game by changing the rules are often underappreciated. If negotiations in your business take place without rules, consider how bringing in a new rule would change the game. But be careful. Just as you can rewrite rules and make new ones, so, too, can others. Unlike other games, business has no ultimate rule-

making authority to settle disputes. History matters.
The government can make some rules—through
antitrust laws, for example. In the end, however, the
power to make rules comes largely from power in the
marketplace. While it's true that rules can trump added
value, it is added value that confers the power to make
rules in the first place. As they said in the old West, "A
Smith & Wesson beats a straight flush."

## Tactics: Changing Perceptions

We've changed the players, their added values, and the
rules. Is there anything left to change? Yes—perceptions.
There is no guarantee that everyone agrees on who the
players are, what their added values are, and what the
rules are. Nor are the implications of every move and
countermove likely to be clear. Business is mired in
uncertainty. Tactics influence the way players perceive
the uncertainty and thus mold their behavior. Some tactics work by reducing misperceptions—in other words,
by lifting the fog. Others work by creating or maintaining uncertainty—by thickening the fog.

Here we offer two examples. The first shows how
Rupert Murdoch lifted the fog to influence how the *New
York Daily News* perceived the game; the second illustrates how maintaining a fog can help negotiating parties reach an agreement.

### THE NEW YORK FOG

In the beginning of July 1994, the *Daily News* raised its
price from 40 cents to 50 cents. This seemed rather
remarkable under the circumstances. Its major rival,
Rupert Murdoch's *New York Post*, was test-marketing a

price cut to 25 cents and had demonstrated its effectiveness on Staten Island. As the *New York Times* saw it (Press Notes, July 4), it was as if the *Daily News* were daring Murdoch to follow through with his price cut.

But, in fact, there was more going on than the *Times* realized. Murdoch had earlier raised the price of the *Post* to 50 cents, and the *Daily News* had held at 40 cents. As a result, the *Post* was losing subscribers and, with them, advertising revenue. Whereas Murdoch viewed the situation as unsustainable, the *Daily News* didn't see any problem—or at least appeared not to. A convenient fog.

Murdoch came up with a tactic to try to lift the fog. Instead of just lowering his price back down to 40 cents, he announced his intention to lower it to 25 cents. The people at the *Daily News* doubted that Murdoch could afford to pull it off. Moreover, they believed that their recent success was due to a superior product and not just to the dime price advantage. They were not particularly threatened by Murdoch's announcement.

Seeing no response, Murdoch tried a second tactic. He started the price reduction on Staten Island as a test run. As a result, sales of the *Post* doubled—and the fog lifted. The *Daily News* learned that its readers were remarkably willing to read the *Post* in order to save 15 cents. The paper's added value was not so large after all. Suddenly, it didn't seem so stupid for Murdoch to have lowered his price to a quarter. It became clear that disastrous consequences would befall the *Daily News* if Murdoch extended his price cut throughout New York City. In London, just such a meltdown scenario was taking place between Murdoch's *Times* and Conrad Black's *Daily Telegraph*. It was in the context of all these events that the *Daily News* raised its price to 50 cents.

Only the *New York Times* remained in a fog. Murdoch had never wanted to lower his price to 25 cents. He never would have expected the *Daily News* to stay at 40 cents had he initiated an across-the-board cut to 25 cents. Murdoch's announcement and the test run on Staten Island were simply tactics designed to get the *Daily News* to raise its price. With price parity, the *Post* no longer would be losing subscribers, and both papers would be more profitable than if they were priced at 25 cents or even at 40 cents. Coopetition strikes again. The *Post* took an initial hit in raising its price to 50 cents, and when the *Daily News* tried to be greedy and not follow suit, Murdoch showed it the light. When the *Daily News* raised its price, it was not daring Murdoch at all. It was saving itself—and Murdoch—from a price war.

In the case of the *Daily News* and the *Post*, the fog was convenient to the former but not to the latter. So Murdoch lifted it.

## DISAGREEING TO AGREE

Sometimes, a fog is convenient to all parties. A fee negotiation between an investment bank and its client (a composite of several confidential negotiations) offers a good example. The client is a company whose owners are forced to sell. The investment bank has identified a potential acquirer. So far, the investment bank has been working on good faith, and now it's time to sign a fee letter.

The investment bank suggests a 1% fee. The client figures that its company will fetch $500 million and argues that a $5 million fee would be excessive. It proposes a 0.625% fee. The investment bankers think that the price will be closer to $250 million and that accepting the client's proposal would cut their expected fee from $2.5 million to about $1.5 million.

One tactic would be to lift the fog. The investment bank could try to convince the client that a $500 million valuation is unrealistic and that its fear of a $5 million fee is therefore unfounded. The problem with this tactic is that the client does not want to hear a low valuation. Faced with such a prospect, it might walk away from the deal and even from the bank altogether—and then there would be no fee.

The client's optimism and the investment bankers' pessimism create an opportunity for an agreement rather than an argument. Both sides should agree to a 0.625% fee combined with a $2.5 million guarantee. That way, the client gets the percentage it wants and considers the guarantee a throwaway. With a 0.625% fee, the guarantee kicks in only for a sales price below $400 million, and the client expects the price to be $100 million higher. Because the investment bankers expected $2.5 million under their original proposal, now that this fee is guaranteed, they can agree to a lower percentage.

Negotiating over pure percentage fees is inherently win-lose. If the fee falls from 1% to 0.625%, the client wins and the investment bankers lose. Going from 1% to 0.625% plus a floor is win-win—but only when the two parties maintain different perceptions. The fog allows for coopetition.

## Changing the Scope

After players, added values, rules, and tactical possibilities, there is nothing left to change within the existing boundaries of the game. But no game is an island.

Games are linked across space and over time. A game in one place can affect games elsewhere, and a game today can influence games tomorrow. You can change the scope of a game. You can expand it by creating linkages to other games, or you can shrink it by severing linkages. Either approach may work to your benefit.

We left Nintendo with a stock market value exceeding both Sony's and Nissan's, and with Mario better known than Mickey Mouse. Sega and other would-be rivals had failed in the 8-bit game. But while the rest fell by the wayside, Sega didn't give up. It introduced a new 16-bit system to the U.S. market. It took two years before Nintendo responded with its own 16-bit machine. By then, with the help of its game hero, Sonic the Hedgehog, Sega had established a secure and significant market position. Today the two companies roughly split the 16-bit market.

Was Sega lucky to get such a long, uncontested period in which to establish itself? Did Nintendo simply blow it? We think not. Nintendo's 8-bit franchise was still very valuable. Sega realized that by expanding the scope, it could turn Nintendo's 8-bit strength into a 16-bit weakness. Put yourself in Nintendo's shoes: Would you jump into the 16-bit game or hold back? Had Nintendo jumped into the game, it would have meant competition and, hence, lower 16-bit prices. Lower prices for 16-bit games, substitutes for 8-bit games, would have reduced the value created by the 8-bit games—a big hit to Nintendo's bottom line. Letting Sega have the 16-bit market all to itself meant that 16-bit prices were higher than they otherwise would have been. Higher 16-bit prices cushioned the effect of the new-generation technology on the old. By staying out of Sega's way, Nintendo made a calculated trade-off: Give up a piece of the 16-bit action in order to extend the life of the 8-bit market. Nintendo's decision to hold back was reasonable, given the link between 8-bit and 16-bit games. Note that the decision not to create competition in a substitutes market is the mirror image of 3DO's strategy of creating competition in a complements market.

## The Traps of Strategy

Changing the game is hard. There are many potential traps. Our mind-set, map, and method for changing the game—coopetition, the Value Net, and PARTS—are designed to help managers recognize and avoid these traps.

The first mental trap is to think you have to accept the game you find yourself in. Just realizing that you can change the game is crucial. There's more work to be done, but it's far more rewarding to be a game maker than a game taker.

The next trap is to think that changing the game must come at the expense of others. Such thinking can lead to an embattled mind-set that causes you to miss win-win opportunities. The coopetition mind-set—looking for both win-win and win-lose strategies—is far more rewarding.

Another trap is to believe that you have to find something to do that others can't. When you do come up with a way to change the game, accept that your actions might well be imitated. Being unique is not a prerequisite for success. Imitation can be healthy, as the GM card story and others illustrate.

The fourth trap is failing to see the whole game. What you don't see, you can't change. In particular, many people overlook the role of complementors. The solution is to draw the Value Net for your business; it will double your repertoire of strategies for changing the game. Any strategy toward customers has a counterpart with suppliers (and vice versa), and any strategy with substitutors has a mirror image for complementors (and vice versa).

The fifth trap is failing to think methodically about changing the game. Using PARTS as a comprehensive, theory-based set of levers helps generate strategies, but that is not enough. To understand the effect of any particular strategy, you need to go beyond your own perspective. Be allocentric, not egocentric.

For the Holland Sweetener Company, it would have helped to recognize that Coke and Pepsi would have paid a high price up front to make the aspartame market competitive. BellSouth succeeded with a weak hand only because it understood the incentives of Lin and McCaw. Nintendo's power in the 8-bit game came from lowering everyone else's added value. To craft the right choice of capacity and price, Kiwi had to put itself in the shoes of the major airlines to ensure that they would have a greater incentive to accommodate rather than fight Kiwi's entry. The effect of a meet-the-competition clause becomes clear only after you consider how a challenger thinks you would respond to an attempt it might make to steal one of your customers. To achieve his ends, Murdoch had to recognize that the *Daily News* was in a fog and find a way to lift it. By understanding how different parties perceive the game differently, a negotiator is better able to forge an agreement. Sega's success depended on the dilemma it created for Nintendo by starting a new 16-bit game linked to the existing 8-bit game.

Finally, there is no silver bullet for changing the game of business. It is an ongoing process. Others will be trying to change the game, too. Sometimes their changes will work to your benefit and sometimes not. You may

need to change the game again. There is, after all, no end
to the game of changing the game.

## Notes

1. In-depth discussion and applications of the principle of
   looking forward and reasoning backward are provided in
   *Thinking Strategically: The Competitive Edge in Business,
   Politics, and Everyday Life*, by Avinash Dixit and Barry
   Nalebuff (W.W. Norton, 1991).

2. The argument is spelled out in Adam Brandenburger and
   Harborne Stuart, "Value-based Business Strategy," which
   will appear in a forthcoming issue of *Journal of Economics
   & Management Strategy*.

3. This portmanteau word can be traced to Ray Noorda,
   CEO of Novell, who has used it to describe relationships
   in the information technology business: "You have to
   cooperate and compete at the same time" (*Electronic
   Business Buyer*, December 1993).

4. McCaw paid $26.5 million to Los Angeles RCC—a joint
   venture between McCaw and BellSouth that was 85%
   owned by BellSouth. Since McCaw did not get any additional equity for his investment, it was in essence a $22.5
   million payment to BellSouth and a $4 million payment to
   himself. Security laws override antitrust laws, so it's legal
   for one bidder to pay another not to be a player.

5. Unfortunately, the program provided little comfort to
   Cozzi, who resigned when TWA scaled it back. TWA
   returned to full-scale Comfort Class in the fall of 1994.

6. On a separate issue, Nintendo made a settlement with the
   Federal Trade Commission in which it agreed to stop
   requiring retailers to adhere to a minimum price for the

game console. Further, Nintendo would give previous buyers a $5-off coupon toward future purchases of Nintendo game cartridges. Reflecting on the case, *Barron's* suggested that "the legion of trust-busting lawyers would be far more productively occupied playing Super Mario Brothers 3 than bringing cases of this kind" (December 3, 1991).

**Originally published in July–August 1995**
**Reprint 95402**

*The authors are grateful to F. William Barnett, Putnam Coes, Amy Guggenheim, Michael Maples, Anna Minto, Troy Paredes, Harborne Stuart, Bart Troyer, Michael Tuchen, and Peter Wetenhall, along with many other colleagues and students, for their generous comments and suggestions.*

# Discovery-Driven Planning

RITA GUNTHER MCGRATH AND

IAN C. MACMILLAN

## Executive Summary

BUSINESS LORE IS FULL OF STORIES about smart companies incurring huge losses when they enter unknown territory—new alliances, markets, products, technologies. Failures could be prevented or their cost contained if managers approached innovative ventures with the right planning and control tools.

Discovery-driven planning is a practical tool that acknowledges the difference between planning for a new venture and for a more conventional business. New ventures are undertaken with a high ratio of assumption to knowledge. But assumptions about the unknown are often wrong. New ventures inevitably experience deviations—often huge ones—from their original targets. Indeed, new ventures frequently require fundamental redirection.

Rather than trying to force start-ups into the planning methodologies for existing, well-understood businesses, the authors offer managers a tool that highlights potentially dangerous implicit assumptions. Discovery-driven planning converts assumptions into knowledge as a strategic venture unfolds.

Using Kao Corporation's entry into floppy disks, the authors present a step-by-step approach to help companies think differently about planning. Managers should begin with the bottom line and work their way up the income statement, first determining a new venture's profit potential.

When a significant strategic undertaking is fraught with uncertainty, discovery-driven planning is an especially powerful tool. It forces managers to articulate what they don't know and provides a discipline to help them address—before making major resource commitments—the make-or-break unknowns common to new ventures.

---

$B$USINESS LORE IS FULL OF STORIES about smart companies that incur huge losses when they enter unknown territory—new alliances, new markets, new products, new technologies. The Walt Disney Company's 1992 foray into Europe with its theme park had accumulated losses of more than $1 billion by 1994. Zapmail, a fax product, cost Federal Express Corporation $600 million before it was dropped. Polaroid lost $200 million when it ventured into instant movies. Why do such efforts often defeat even experienced, smart companies? One obvious answer is that strategic ventures are inherently risky: The probability of failure simply comes with the territory. But many failures could be prevented or their cost contained if senior managers approached innovative ventures with the right planning and control tools.

Discovery-driven planning is a practical tool that acknowledges the difference between planning for a new venture and planning for a more conventional line of business. Conventional

*Discovery-driven planning recognizes that planning for a new venture involves envisioning the unknown.*

planning operates on the premise that managers can extrapolate future results from a well-understood and predictable platform of past experience. One expects predictions to be accurate because they are based on solid knowledge rather than on assumptions. In platform-based planning, a venture's deviations from plan are a bad thing.

The platform-based approach may make sense for ongoing businesses, but it is sheer folly when applied to new ventures. By definition, new ventures call for a company to envision what is unknown, uncertain, and not yet obvious to the competition. The safe, reliable, predictable knowledge of the well-understood business has not yet emerged. Instead, managers must make do with assumptions about the possible futures on which new businesses are based. New ventures are undertaken with a high ratio of assumption to knowledge. With ongoing businesses, one expects the ratio to be the exact opposite. Because assumptions about the unknown generally turn out to be wrong, new ventures inevitably experience deviations—often huge ones—from their original planned targets. Indeed, new ventures frequently require fundamental redirection.

Rather than trying to force start-ups into the planning methodologies for existing predictable and well-understood businesses, discovery-driven planning acknowledges that at the start of a new venture, little is known and much is assumed. When platform-based planning is used, assumptions underlying a plan are treated as facts—givens to be baked into the plan—rather than as best-guess estimates to be tested and questioned. Companies then forge ahead on the basis of those buried assumptions. In contrast, discovery-driven planning systematically converts assumptions into knowledge as a strategic venture unfolds. When new data are uncovered, they are incorporated into the evolving plan. The real potential of the venture is discovered as it develops—hence the term discovery-driven planning. The approach imposes disciplines different from, but no less precise than, the disciplines used in conventional planning.

## Euro Disney and the Platform-Based Approach

Even the best companies can run into serious trouble if they don't recognize the assumptions buried in their plans. The Walt Disney Company, a 49% owner of Euro Disney (now called Disneyland Paris), is known as an astute manager of theme parks. Its success has not been confined to the United States: Tokyo Disneyland has been a financial and public relations success almost from its opening in 1983. Euro Disney is another story, however. By 1993, attendance approached 1 million visitors each month, making the park Europe's most popular paid tourist destination. Then why did it lose so much money?

In planning Euro Disney in 1986, Disney made projections that drew on its experience from its other parks. The company expected half of the revenue to come from admissions, the other half from hotels, food, and merchandise. Although by 1993, Euro Disney had succeeded in reaching its target of 11 million admissions, to do so it had been forced to drop adult ticket prices drastically. The average spending per visit was far below plan and added to the red ink.

The point is not to play Monday-morning quarterback with Disney's experience but to demonstrate an approach that could have revealed flawed assumptions and mitigated the resulting losses. The discipline of systematically identifying key assumptions would have highlighted the business plan's vulnerabilities. Let us look at each source of revenue in turn.

## ADMISSIONS PRICE

In Japan and the United States, Disney found its price by raising it over time, letting early visitors go back home and talk up the park to their neighbors. But the planners of Euro Disney assumed that they could hit their target number of visitors even if they started out with an admission price of more than $40 per adult. A major recession in Europe and the determination of the French government to keep the franc strong exacerbated the problem and led to low attendance. Although companies cannot control macroeconomic events, they can highlight and test their pricing assumptions. Euro Disney's prices were very high compared with those of other theme attractions in Europe, such as the aqua palaces, which charged low entry fees and allowed visitors to build their own menus by paying for each attraction individually. By 1993, Euro Disney not only had been forced to make a sharp price reduction to secure its target visitors, it had also lost the benefits of early-stage word of mouth. The talking-up phenomenon is especially important in Europe, as Disney could have gauged from the way word of mouth had benefited Club Med.

## HOTEL ACCOMMODATIONS

Based on its experience in other markets, Disney assumed that people would stay an average of four days in the park's five hotels. The average stay in 1993 was only two days. Had the assumption been highlighted, it might have been challenged: Since Euro Disney opened with only 15 rides, compared with 45 at Disney World, people could do them all in a single day.

*Euro Disney assumed that Europeans would "graze" all day, like visitors to other Disney parks.*

## FOOD

Park visitors in the United States and Japan "graze" all day. At Euro Disney, the buried assumption was that Europeans would do the same. Euro Disney's restaurants, therefore, were designed for all-day streams of grazers. When floods of visitors tried to follow the European custom of dining at noon, Disney was unable to seat them. Angry visitors left the park to eat, and they conveyed their anger to their friends and neighbors back home.

## MERCHANDISE

Although Disney did forecast lower sales per visitor in Europe than in the United States and Japan, the company assumed that Europeans would buy a similar mix of cloth goods and print items. Instead, Euro Disney fell short of plan when visitors bought a far smaller proportion of high-margin items such as T-shirts and hats than expected. Disney could have tested the buried assumption before forecasting sales: Disney's retail stores in European cities sell many fewer of the high-margin cloth items and far more of the low-margin print items.

*Companies can learn to spot when they're making unconscious assumptions.*

Disney is not alone. Other companies have paid a significant price for pursuing platform-based ventures built on implicit assumptions that turn out to be faulty. Such ventures are usually undertaken without careful up-front identification and validation of those assumptions, which often are unconscious. We have repeatedly observed that the following four planning errors are characteristic of this approach:

- *Companies don't have hard data but, once a few key decisions are made, proceed as though their assumptions were facts.* Euro Disney's implicit assumptions regarding the way visitors would use hotels and restaurants are good examples.

- *Companies have all the hard data they need to check assumptions but fail to see the implications.* After making assumptions based on a subset of the available data, they proceed without ever testing those assumptions. Federal Express based Zapmail on the assumption that there would be a substantial demand for four-hour delivery of documents faxed from FedEx center to FedEx center. What went unchallenged was the implicit assumption that customers would not be able to afford their own fax machines before long. If that assumption had been unearthed, FedEx would have been more likely to take into account the plunging prices and increasing sales of fax machines for the office and, later, for the home.

- *Companies possess all the data necessary to determine that a real opportunity exists but make implicit and inappropriate assumptions about their ability to implement their plan.* Exxon lost $200 million on its office automation business by implicitly assuming that it could build a direct sales and service support capability to compete head-to-head with IBM and Xerox.

- *Companies start off with the right data, but they implicitly assume a static environment and thus fail to notice until too late that a key variable has changed.* Polaroid lost $200 million from Polavision instant movies by assuming that a three-minute cassette costing $7 would compete effectively against a half-hour videotape costing $20. Polaroid implicitly assumed that the high cost of equipment for video-taping and playback would remain prohibitive for most consumers. Meanwhile, companies pursuing those technologies steadily drove down costs. (See the exhibit "Some Dangerous Implicit Assumptions.")

## Discovery-Driven Planning: An Illustrative Case

Discovery-driven planning offers a systematic way to uncover the dangerous implicit assumptions that would otherwise slip unnoticed and thus unchallenged into the plan. The process imposes a strict discipline that is captured in four related documents: a *reverse income statement*, which models the basic economics of the business;

---

### Some Dangerous Implicit Assumptions

1. Customers will buy our product because we think it's a good product.

2. Customers will buy our product because it's technically superior.

3. Customers will agree with our perception that the product is "great."

4. Customers run no risk in buying from us instead of continuing to buy from their past suppliers.

5. The product will sell itself.

6. Distributors are desperate to stock and service the product.

7. We can develop the product on time and on budget.

8. We will have no trouble attracting the right staff.

9. Competitors will respond rationally.

10. We can insulate our product from competition.

11. We will be able to hold down prices while gaining share rapidly.

12. The rest of our company will gladly support our strategy and provide help as needed.

*pro forma operations specs*, which lay out the operations needed to run the business; a *key assumptions checklist*, which is used to ensure that assumptions are checked; and a *milestone planning chart*, which specifies the assumptions to be tested at each project milestone. As the venture unfolds and new data are uncovered, each of the documents is updated.

To demonstrate how this tool works, we will apply it retrospectively to Kao Corporation's highly successful entry into the floppy disk business in 1988. We deliberately draw on no inside information about Kao or its planning process but instead use the kind of limited public knowledge that often is all that any company would have at the start of a new venture.

## THE COMPANY

Japan's Kao Corporation was a successful supplier of surfactants to the magnetic-media (floppy disk) industry. In 1981, the company began to study the potential for becoming a player in floppy disks by leveraging the surfactant technology it had developed in its core businesses, soap and cosmetics. Kao's managers realized that they had learned enough process knowledge from their floppy disk customers to supplement their own skills in surface chemistry. They believed they could produce floppy disks at a much lower cost and higher quality than other companies offered at that time. Kao's surfactant competencies were particularly valuable because the quality of the floppy disk's surface is crucial for its reliability. For a company in a mature industry, the opportunity to move current product into a growth industry was highly attractive.

## THE MARKET

By the end of 1986, the demand for floppy disks was 500 million in the United States, 100 million in Europe, and 50 million in Japan, with growth estimated at 40% per year, compounded. This meant that by 1993, the global market would be approaching 3 billion disks, of which about a third would be in the original equipment manufacturer (OEM) market, namely such big-volume purchasers of disks as IBM, Apple, and Microsoft, which use disks to distribute their software. OEM industry prices were expected to be about 180 yen per disk by 1993. Quality and reliability have always been important product characteristics for OEMs such as software houses because defective disks have a devastating impact on customers' perceptions of the company's overall quality.

## THE REVERSE INCOME STATEMENT

Discovery-driven planning starts with the bottom line. For Kao, back when it began to consider its options, the question was whether the floppy disk venture had the potential to enhance the company's competitive position and financial performance significantly. If not, why should Kao incur the risk and uncertainty of a major strategic venture?

Here, we impose the first discipline, which is to plan the venture using a reverse income statement, which runs from the bottom line up. (See page 126, section entitled "First, Start with a Reverse Income Statement.") Instead of starting with estimates of revenues and working down the income statement to derive profits, we start with *required profits*. We then work our way up the profit and loss to determine how much revenue it will take to deliver the level of profits we require and how much cost can be allowed. The underlying philosophy is to impose revenue and cost disciplines by baking profitability into the plan at the outset: Required profits equal necessary revenues minus allowable costs.

At Kao in 1988, management might have started with these figures: net sales, about 500 billion yen; income before taxes, about 40 billion yen; and return on sales (ROS), 7.5%. Given such figures, how big must the floppy disk opportunity be to justify Kao's attention? Every company will set its own hurdles. We believe that a strategic venture should have the potential to enhance total profits by at least 10%. Moreover, to compensate for the increased risk, it should deliver greater profitability than reinvesting in the existing businesses would. Again, for purposes of illustration, assume that Kao demands a risk premium of 33% greater profitability. Since Kao's return on sales is 7.5%, it will require 10%.

*Retrospectively applying discovery-driven planning to KAO's successful 1988 floppy disk venture shows how the tool can work.*

If we use the Kao data, we find that the required profit for the floppy disk venture would be 4 billion yen (10% × 40 billion). To deliver 4 billion yen in profit with a 10% return on sales implies a business with 40 billion yen in sales.

Assuming that, despite its superior quality, Kao will have to price competitively to gain share as a new entrant, it should set a target price of 160 yen per disk. That translates into unit sales of 250 million disks (40 billion yen in sales divided by 160 yen per disk). By imposing these simple performance measures at the start (1988), we quickly establish both the scale and scope of the venture: Kao would need to capture 25% of the total world OEM market (25% of 1 billion disks) by 1993. Given what is known about the size of the market, Kao clearly must be prepared to compete globally from the outset, making major commitments not only to manufacturing but also to selling.

Continuing up the profit and loss, we next calculate allowable costs: If Kao is to capture 10% margin on a price of 160 yen per disk, the total cost to manufacture, sell, and distribute the disks worldwide cannot exceed 144 yen per disk. The reverse income statement makes clear immediately that the challenge for the floppy disk venture will be to keep a lid on expenses.

## THE PRO FORMA OPERATIONS SPECS AND THE ASSUMPTIONS CHECKLIST

The second discipline in the process is to construct pro forma operations specs laying out the activities required to produce, sell, service, and deliver the product or service to the customer. Together, those activities comprise the venture's allowable costs. At first, the operations specs can be modeled on a simple spreadsheet without investing in more than a few telephone calls or on-line searches to get basic data. If an idea holds together, it is possible to identify and test underlying assumptions, constantly fleshing out and correcting the model in light of new information. When a company uses this cumulative approach, major flaws in the business concept soon become obvious, and poor concepts can be abandoned long before significant investments are made.

We believe it is essential to use industry standards for building a realistic picture of what the business has to look like to be competitive. Every industry has its own pressures—which determine normal rates of return in that industry—as well as standard performance measures such as asset-to-sales ratios, industry profit margins, plant utilization, and so on. In a globally competitive environment, no sane manager should expect to escape the competitive discipline that is captured and measured in industry standards. These standards are readily available from investment analysts and business information services. In countries with information sources that are less well developed than those in the United States, key industry parameters are still used by investment bankers and, more specifically, by those commercial bankers who specialize in loans to the particular industry. For those getting into a new industry, the best approach is to adapt standards from similar industries.

Note that we do not begin with an elaborate analysis of product or service attributes or an in-depth market study. That comes later. Initially, we are simply trying to capture the venture's embedded assumptions. The basic discipline is to spell out clearly and realistically where the venture will have to match existing industry standards and in what one or two places managers expect to excel and how they expect to do so.

Kao's managers in 1988 might have considered performance standards for the floppy disk industry. Because there would be no reason to believe that Kao could use standard production equipment any better than established competitors could, it would want to plan to match industry performance on measures relating to equipment use. Kao would ascertain, for example, that the effective production capacity per line was 25 disks per minute in the industry; and the effective life of production equipment was three years. Kao's advantage was in surface chemistry and surface physics, which could improve quality and reduce the cost of materials, thus improving margins. When Kao planned its materials cost, it would want to turn that advantage into a specific challenge for manufacturing: Beat the industry standard for materials cost by 25%. The formal framing of operational challenges

*Unearthing implicit assumptions permits a company to test their validity before committing irreversibly to a venture.*

is an important step in discovery-driven planning. In our experience, people who are good in design and operations can be galvanized by clearly articulated challenges. That was the case at Canon, for example, when Keizo Yamaji challenged the engineers to develop a personal copier that required minimal service and cost less than $1,000, and the Canon engineers rose to the occasion.

A company can test the initial assumptions against experience with similar situations, the advice of experts in the industry, or published information sources. The point is not to demand the highest degree of accuracy but to build a reasonable model of the economics and logistics of the venture and to assess the order of magnitude of the challenges. Later, the company can analyze where the plan is most sensitive to wrong assumptions and do more formal checks. Consultants to the industry—bankers, suppliers, potential customers, and distributors—often can provide low-cost and surprisingly accurate information.

The company must build a picture of the activities that are needed to carry out the business and the costs. Hence in the pro forma operations specs, we ask how many orders are needed to deliver 250 million units in sales; then how many sales calls it will take to secure those orders; then how many salespeople it will take to make the sales calls, given the fact that they are selling to a global OEM market; then how much it will cost in sales-force compensation. (See page 126, section entitled "Second, Lay Out All the Activities Needed to Run the Venture.") Each assumption can be checked, at first somewhat roughly and then with increasing precision. Readers might disagree with our first-cut estimates. That is fine—so might Kao Corporation. Reasonable disagreement triggers discussion and, perhaps, adjustments to the spreadsheet. The evolving document is doing its job if it becomes the catalyst for such discussion.

The third discipline of discovery-driven planning is to compile an assumption checklist to ensure that each assumption is flagged, discussed, and checked as the venture unfolds. (See page 127, section entitled "Third, Track All Assumptions.")

The entire process is looped back into a revised reverse income statement, in which one can see if the entire business proposition hangs together. (See page 128, section entitled, "Fourth, Revise the Reverse Income Statement.") If it doesn't, the process must be repeated until the performance requirements and industry standards can be met; otherwise, the venture should be scrapped.

**Milestone Planning.** Conventional planning approaches tend to focus managers on meeting plan, usually an impossible goal for a venture rife with assumptions. It is also counterproductive—insistence on meeting plan actually prevents learning. Managers can formally plan to learn by using milestone events to test assumptions.

Milestone planning is by now a familiar technique for monitoring the progress of new ventures. The basic idea, as described by Zenas Block and Ian C. MacMillan in the book *Corporate Venturing* (Harvard Business School Press, 1993), is to postpone major commitments of resources until the evidence from the previous milestone event signals that the risk of taking the next step is justified. What we are proposing here is an expanded use of the tool to support the discipline of transforming assumptions into knowledge.

Going back to what Kao might have been thinking in 1988, recall that the floppy disk venture would require a 40-billion-yen investment in fixed assets alone. Before investing such a large sum, Kao would certainly have wanted to find ways to test the most critical assumptions underlying the three major challenges of the venture:

- capturing 25% global market share with a 20-yen-per-disk discount and superior quality;

- maintaining at least the same asset productivity as the average competitor and producing a floppy disk at 90% of the estimated total costs of existing competitors; and

• using superior raw materials and applied surface technology to produce superior-quality disks for 20 yen per unit instead of the industry standard of 27 yen per unit.

For serious challenges like those, it may be worth spending resources to create specific milestone events to test the assumptions before launching a 40-billion-yen venture. For instance, Kao might subcontract prototype production so that sophisticated OEM customers could conduct technical tests on the proposed disk. If the prototypes survive the tests, then, rather than rest on the assumption that it can capture significant business at the target price, Kao might subcontract production of a large batch of floppy disks for resale to customers. It could thus test the appetite of the OEM market for price discounting from a newcomer.

Similarly, for testing its ability to cope with the second and third challenges once the Kao prototype has been developed, it might be worthwhile to buy out a small existing floppy disk manufacturer and apply the technology in an established plant rather than try to start up a greenfield operation. Once Kao can demonstrate its ability to produce disks at the required quality and cost in the small plant, it can move ahead with its own full-scale plants.

Deliberate assumption-testing milestones are depicted on page 128, in the section entitled "Finally, Plan to Test Assumptions at Milestones," which also shows some of the other typical milestones that occur in most major ventures. The assumptions that should be tested at each milestone are listed with appropriate numbers from the assumption checklist.

In practice, it is wise to designate a *keeper of the assumptions*—someone whose formal task is to ensure that assumptions are checked and updated as each milestone is reached and that the revised assumptions are incorporated into successive iterations of the four discovery-driven planning documents. Without a specific person dedicated to following up, it is highly unlikely that individuals, up to their armpits in project pressures, will be able to coordinate the updating independently.

D ISCOVERY-DRIVEN PLANNING is a powerful tool for any significant strategic undertaking that is fraught with uncertainty—new-product or market ventures, technology development, joint ventures, strategic alliances, even major systems redevelopment. Unlike platform-based planning, in which much is known, discovery-driven planning forces managers to articulate what they don't know, and it forces a discipline for learning. As a planning tool, it thus raises the visibility of the make-or-break uncertainties common to new ventures and helps managers address them at the lowest possible cost.

# How Kao Might Have Tackled Its New Venture: Discovery-Driven Planning in Action

## First, Start with a Reverse Income Statement

*The goal here is to determine the value of success quickly. If the venture can't deliver significant returns, it may not be worth the risk.*

### Total Figures
Required profits to add 10% to total profits = 4 billion yen
Necessary revenues to deliver 10% sales margin = 40 billion yen
Allowable costs to deliver 10% sales margin = 36 billion yen

### Per Unit Figures
Required unit sales at 160 yen per unit = 250 million units
Necessary percentage of world market share of OEM unit sales = 25%
Allowable costs per unit for 10% sales margin = 144 yen

---

## Second, Lay Out All the Activities Needed to Run the Venture

### Pro Forma Operations Specs

### 1. Sales
Required disk sales = 250 million disks
Average order size (Assumption 8) = 10,000 disks
Orders required (250 million/10,000, = 25,000

Number of calls to make a sale (Assumption 9) = 4
Sales calls required (4 × 25,000) = 100,000 per year

Calls per day per salesperson (Assumption 10) = 2
Annual salesperson days (100,000/2) = 50,000
Sales force for 250 days per year (Assumption 11)
    50,000 salesperson days/250 = 200 people

Salary per salesperson = 10 million yen (Assumption 12)
    Total sales-force salary cost (10 million yen × 200) = 2 billion yen

### 2. Manufacturing
Quality specification of disk surface: 50% fewer
    flaws than best competitor (Assumption 15)

Annual production capacity per line = 25 per minute
    × 1440 minutes per day × 348 days (Assumption 16) = 12.5 million disks
Production lines needed (250 million disks/12.5 million disks per line) = 20 lines

Production staffing (30 per line [Assumption 17] × 20 line) = 600 workers

Salary per worker = 5 million yen (Assumption 18)
Total production salaries (600 × 5 million yen) = 3 billion yen

Materials costs per disk = 20 yen (Assumption 19)
Total materials cost (20 × 250 million disks) = 5 billion yen
Packaging per 10 disks = 40 yen (Assumption 20)
Total packaging costs (40 × 25 million packages) = 1 billion yen

### 3. Shipping
Containers needed per order of 10,000 disks = 1 (Assumption 13)
Shipping cost per container = 100,000 yen (Assumption 14)
Total shipping costs (25,000 orders × 100,000 yen) = 2.5 billion yen

### 4. Equipment and Depreciation
Fixed asset investment to sales = 1:1 (Assumption 5) = 40 billion yen
Equipment life = 3 years (Assumption 7)
Annual depreciation (40 billion yen/3 years) = 13.3 billion yen

## Third, Track All Assumptions

*Keeping a checklist is an important discipline to ensure that each assumption is flagged and tested as a venture unfolds.*

| Assumption | Measurment |
|---|---|
| 1. Profit margin | 10% of sales |
| 2. Revenues | 40 billion yen |
| 3. Unit selling price | 160 yen |
| 4. 1993 world OEM market | 1 billion disks |
| 5. Fixed asset investment to sales | 1:1 |
| 6. Effective production capacity per line | 25 disks per minute |
| 7. Effective life of equipment | 3 years |
| 8. Average OEM order size | 10,000 disks |
| 9. Sales calls per OEM order | 4 calls per order |
| 10. Sales calls per salesperson per day | 2 calls per day |
| 11. Selling days per year | 250 days |
| 12. Annual salesperson's salary | 10 million yen |
| 13. Containers required per order | 1 container |
| 14. Shipping cost per container | 100,000 yen |
| 15. Quality level needed to get customers to switch: % fewer flaws per disks than top competitor | 50% |
| 16. Production days per years | 348 days |
| 17. Workers per production line per day (10 per line for 3 shifts) | 30 per line |
| 18. Annual manufacturing worker's salary | 5 million yen |

| | |
|---|---|
| **19.** Materials costs per disk | 20 yen |
| **20.** Packaging costs per 10 disks | 40 yen |
| **21.** Allowable administration costs<br>(See revised reverse income statement, below) | 9.2 billion yen |

## Fourth, Revise the Reverse Income Statement

*Now, with better data, one can see if the entire business proposition hangs together.*

| | |
|---|---|
| **Required margin** | 10% return on sales |
| **Required profit** | 4 billion yen |
| **Necessary revenues** | 40 billion yen |
| **Allowable costs** | 36 billion yen |
| | |
| Sales-force salaries | 2.0 billion yen |
| Manufacturing salaries | 3.0 billion yen |
| Disk materials | 5.0 billion yen |
| Packaging | 1.0 billion yen |
| Shipping | 2.5 billion yen |
| Depreciation | 13.3 billion yen |
| Allowable administration<br>and overhead costs | 9.2 billion yen (Assumption 21) |

| **Per-unit figures** | |
|---|---|
| Selling price | 160 yen |
| Total costs | 144 yen |
| Disk materials costs | 20 yen |

## Finally, Plan to Test Assumptions at Milestones

| **Milestone event—namely,<br>the completion of:** | **Assumptions to be tested** |
|---|---|
| **1.** Initial data search and pre-<br>liminary feasibility analysis | 4: 1993 world OEM market |
| | 8: Average OEM order size |
| | 9: Sales calls per OEM order |
| | 10: Sales calls per salesperson<br>per day |
| | 11: Salespeople needed for 250<br>selling days per year |
| | 12: Annual salesperson's salary |
| | 13: Containers required per order |
| | 14: Shipping cost per container |
| | 16: Production days per years |
| | 18: Annual manufacturing<br>worker's salary |
| **2.** Prototype batches produced | 15: Quality to get customers<br>to switch |
| | 19: Materials costs per disk |

**3.** Technical testing by
customers

3: Unit selling price
15: Quality to get customers
to switch

**4.** Subcontracted production

19: Materials costs per disk

**5.** Sales of subcontracted
production

1: Profit margin
2: Revenues
3: Unit selling price
8: Average OEM order size
9: Sales calls per OEM order
10: Sales calls per salesperson
per day
12: Annual salesperson's salary
15: Quality to get customers
to switch

**Originally published in July–August 1995**
**Reprint 95406**

*The authors wish to thank Shiuchi Matsuda of Waseda University's
Entrepreneurial Research Unit for providing case material on Kao's
floppy disk venture.*

# Decision Making

## Going Forward in Reverse

HILLEL J. EINHORN AND

ROBIN M. HOGARTH

## Executive Summary

ALL DECISIONS ARE ABOUT THE FUTURE. But deciding
what to do and how to do it naturally draws on past
experience. Looking foward involves looking backward.
This is so natural that we don't even think about it. But
a better understanding of the direction of thought patterns can help avoid the mental traps that produce bad
decisions.

Does sex cause pregnancy? Do sunspots explain
changes in the stock market? Does daylight cause the
sun to rise? Thinking backward is intuitive and diagnostic. When you think in reverse, you look for patterns,
make judgments that link events, and search for
metaphors and theories that help explain causes and
effects.

When you weigh variables and make calculations
and forecasts based on them, you are thinking forward.

To help prepare alternative plans, you assess whether one event or another will take place. Is a recession likely to occur? What are the options for dealing with it?.

You can think backward better if you use more than one metaphor to describe a situation, resist the temptation to infer a cause from just one clue, and sometimes look for an unexpected cause to explain an effect.

You will think forward better if you learn to use and trust the kinds of computations and models that computers use, for example, more than your own mind. Even though models make errors, you can make good use of them by understanding the kinds of errors they are likely to make and then compensating for them.

---

Busy managers analyze many situations and make hundreds of decisions every day. Why, for example, are sales up in one city but down in another? Would an investment in new equipment mean higher productivity or greater confusion? Is now a good time to look for a joint venture partner, or is it better to wait? Rarely, however, do we stop to think about how we think. Each decision is the outcome of a complex process that usually involves two different kinds of thinking: looking backward to understand the past and looking forward to predict the future.

Thinking backward is largely intuitive and suggestive; it tends to be diagnostic and requires judgment. It involves looking for patterns, making links between seemingly unconnected events, testing possible chains of causation to explain an event, and finding a metaphor or a theory to help in looking forward.

Thinking forward is different. Instead of intuition, it depends on a kind of mathematical formulation: the decision maker must assemble and weigh a number of variables and then make a prediction. Using a strategy or a rule, assessing the accuracy of each factor, and combining all the pieces of information, the decision maker arrives at a single, integrated forecast.

Although managers use both types of thinking all the time, they are often unaware of the differences. Moreover, this lack of awareness makes decision makers stumble into mental traps that yield bad decisions. By understanding thinking backward and forward, we can recognize these traps and improve our decisions.

## Thinking Backward

To understand how thinking backward works, think back to the days of the cave dwellers and consider the following exercise in assessing cause and effect. Imagine that you belong to a tribe that is sophisticated in methodology but primitive in science. Your tribe has very little knowledge of biology, physics, or chemistry but a very big problem—an alarming decrease in the birthrate. The problem is so severe that the tribe's statistician estimates that unless you can reverse the trend soon, the tribe will become extinct.

To respond to the crisis, the chief urgently launches a project to determine the cause of birth. As a member of the project team assigned the task of linking cause and effect, you have been assured that you will be allowed any and all forms of experimentation, including the use of your fellow tribespersons, to resolve this critical issue.

The first question, of course, is what to consider a relevant causal factor. In searching for a link between cause and effect, most people usually look first to some unusual or remarkable event or condition that preceded the effect. In this case, you might ask yourself if something unusual happened before the decline in births. You might look for evidence of the cause of the problem that is similar in some way to the outcome—similar in some physical or metaphorical way. Then you could assess the likelihood that the evidence explains the problem.

You might notice that the children in your tribe are similar in appearance to men and women who live together. This similarity could lead you to a leap of intuition backward: sexual intercourse causes pregnancy. You and the members of your study team would probably acknowledge, however, that this theory is unproven, indeed unsupported. First, there's a big gap between cause and effect—nine months, to be exact. Second, you have no knowledge of the sequence of biological processes that link intercourse and pregnancy, no knowledge of the causal chain. Third, the cause and the effect are very different in scale and duration. And fourth, many other factors that may correlate with intercourse are difficult to rule out—for example, sitting under a palm tree and holding hands in full moonlight (an explanation once advanced in a letter to "Dear Abby").

There is only one way to settle the issue and save the tribe from extinction: conduct an experiment. From a sample of 200 couples, you assign 100 to test intercourse and 100 to test nonintercourse. After some time, you get the following results: of the 100 couples assigned to test intercourse, 20 became pregnant and 80 did not; of the 100 assigned to test nonintercourse, 5 became pregnant and 95 did not. (These five pregnancies represent a fairly typical measurement error in such data and can be explained by faulty memory, lying, and human frailty.)

With the results in hand, you calculate the correlation between intercourse and pregnancy and find that it is .34. Since this correlation is only modest, you conclude

that intercourse is not a major factor in causing pregnancy. You discard your unsupported theory and press
on for another solution. Could there be something to
that palm tree theory, after all?

## THREE STEPS BACK

This example illustrates the three interrelated phases of
thinking backward: finding relevant variables, linking
them in a causal chain, and assessing the plausibility of
the chain.

The search for an explanation often begins when we
notice that something is different, unusual, or wrong.
Usually, it takes an unexpected event to pique our
curiosity—we are rarely interested in finding out why we
feel "average" or why traffic is flowing "normally." In the
case of our cave dwellers, the declining birthrate is both
unusual and threatening and therefore stimulates reme-
dial action.

The next step is to look for some relevant causal factor, to focus on some abnormal event that resembles the
unusual outcome in a number of ways: it may be similar
in scale, in how long it lasts, or in when it happens. Most
people harbor the notion that similar causes have similar effects. For example, according to "the doctrine of
signatures," adopted in early Western medicine, diseases
are caused or cured by substances that physically resemble them. Thus, a cure for jaundice would be yellow, and
so on. As strange as that may seem, it is also difficult to
imagine how we could search for variables without looking for some kind of similarity between cause and effect.

The search for similarity often involves analogy and
metaphor. In trying to understand how the brain works,
for instance, we can imagine it as a computer, a muscle,

or a sponge. Each metaphor suggests a different way of picturing the brain's processes. A computer suggests information input, storage, retrieval, and computation. A muscle suggests building power through use and loss of strength because of atrophy or the strain of overuse. A sponge suggests the passive absorption of information. The metaphor we choose in describing the brain—or in understanding any link between cause and effect—is critical since it directs attention to one way of thinking.

The search for causally relevant variables goes hand in hand with the consideration of indicators, or "cues to causality," that suggest some probable link between cause and effect. There are four categories of cues: temporal order (causes happen before effects), proximity (causes are generally close to effects in time and space), correlation (causes tend to vary along with effects), and similarity (causes may resemble effects through analogy and metaphor or in length and strength).

These cues to causality do not necessarily prove a link between cause and effect. They do, however, indicate likely directions in which to seek relevant variables and limit the number of scenarios or chains that can be constructed between possible causes and their supposed effects.

How likely is it, for example, that sunspots cause price changes on the stock market? Before you dismiss this as an absurd hypothesis, consider that the eminent nineteenth-century economist William Stanley Jevons believed in such a link. To make this link, you have to construct a causal chain that meets various constraints. For the sake of discussion, let's assume that at a certain time some sunspots did occur before price changes (the temporal order is correct); that when the sun had sunspot activity, there were many price changes (the correlation is positive); and that these price changes occurred six months after sunspot activity (the proximity in time is not very close). The task is to bridge the time lag and distance gap between sunspots and price changes. If you cannot do so, you cannot prove a causal relationship.

Now consider the following chain: sunspots affect weather conditions, which affect agricultural production, which affects economic conditions, which affect profits, which affect stock prices. The cues to causality constrain the possible chains that you can imagine. This constraint is especially important in evaluating the cue of temporal order: for one event to cause another, it must precede it. But the cues of proximity in time and space, of congruity, and of the length and strength of cause and effect also constrain the linkage. The way to bridge the spatial and temporal gaps between the sunspots and the stock market changes is to look for a change in the weather.

Imagine, however, that price changes occur immediately after sunspot activity rather than six months later. The closeness in time between the two events eliminates the link between weather and these economic conditions, which requires a time delay. To link sunspots and price changes, you would have to come up with another scenario that meets the test of proximity in time.

Another test that the cues to causality suggest is incongruity—that is, small causes that yield big effects or big causes that produce small effects. To account for these apparent discrepancies, the causal chain must involve some kind of amplification in the first case and some sort of reduction in the second. When Louis Pasteur advanced the germ theory of disease in the 1800s, for example, it must have seemed incredible to his contemporaries, solely because of the test of incongruity. How could tiny, invisible creatures cause disease, plague, and death? In the absence of scientific information, people saw no causal chain that could amplify such minute causes to such enormous effects.

## BETTER THINKING BACKWARD

Several approaches can improve the way we make thinking backward work in decision making:

1. *Use several metaphors.* Because backward thinking is both intuitive and swift, most people can generate a single metaphor quickly and expand it into an extensive causal chain. But all metaphors are imperfect. When you use them, it is important to remember the old adage that the map is not the territory.

   Using several metaphors can be a guard against prematurely adopting a single model. Instead of focusing on one metaphor, experiment with several. Consider, for example, how you might think about complex organizations such as graduate schools of business. Each metaphor illuminates a different dimension of the subject. You could think of business schools as finishing schools, where students mature appropriately before entering corporate life; as military academies, where students prepare for economic warfare; as monasteries, where students receive indoctrination in economic theology; as diploma mills, where students receive certification; or as job shops, where students are tooled to perform specific tasks.

   Each metaphor illustrates a different factor, an alternative way of thinking. No metaphor by itself is adequate; considering them all provides a more complete picture.

2. *Do not rely on one cue alone.* Inferring causality from just one cue often leads to serious error. Because they relied on a single measure, the cave dwellers diverted their attention from the real cause of pregnancy. Correlation does not always imply causation, nor does causation always imply correlation.

3. *Sometimes go against the cues.* A great benefit of the cues is that they give structure to our perceptions and help us interpret ambiguous information. But there is a trade-off between this structure and novelty and originality. The cues help by directing attention to what is obvious and reducing alternative interpretations. But the hallmark of insights is that they surprise us. One way to promote creative thinking, then, is to go against the cues. When searching for an explanation for a complex outcome, sometimes look for a simple or a dissimilar cause rather than a complex or a similar one.

4. *Assess causal chains.* The way to test potential causes and effects is through a causal chain, but the strength of each chain varies. The chain connecting sunspots and stock prices, for instance, is weak because there are so many links and each is uncertain. In fact, most causal chains are only as strong as their weakest links, and long chains are generally weaker than short ones. But research indicates that people do not always grasp these facts. Many people regard complex scenarios with detailed outcomes as much more coherent—and thus much more likely— than simple ones. It is important to evaluate chains according to the number and strength of their links.

5. *Generate and test alternative explanations.* Most people have a natural aptitude for thinking diagnostically. But one of its drawbacks is that it can lead to superstitions that hold sway for long periods. The history of medicine is full of them. For many years, doctors used bloodletting, for instance, as a popular and presumably scientifically sound cure. Could our most cherished theories about economics and business in time become as obsolete as bloodletting?

Experiments can guard against superstition. To assess the effectiveness of advertising, for example, you could conduct experiments by stopping advertising completely. If it is not feasible to go to such extremes, you could use partial tests, which can give you much useful information: you could stop advertising only in certain areas or for certain periods.

If you can't do such an experiment, you can nevertheless imagine situations in which the effect occurs without the suspected cause. In imaginary scenarios, you can judge causal links. The question under consideration may be whether a particular advertising campaign has caused an increase in sales. By trying to answer the question, Would sales have risen without the advertising campaign? you can get an estimate of the proper link between sales and advertising. A worthwhile experiment would include a second question: Will sales go up if we advertise? By posing these questions in a systematic way, you can get information almost as useful and powerful as what you get from actually trying something out.

## Thinking Forward

Whether we like to acknowledge it or not, most of the time we do a poor job of thinking forward with any accuracy. Evidence gathered in such diverse fields as marriage counseling, bank lending, economic forecasting, and psychological counseling indicates that most human predictions are less accurate than even the simplest statistical models.

Most people have more faith in human judgment, however, than in statistical models. The disadvantages of statistical models compared with human judgment seem obvious. Or so the argument goes. But is this right? Let's consider the evidence.

**Models make errors.** The use of a formal model implies trade-offs; a model will make errors since it is an abstraction that cannot possibly capture the full richness of the relations between variables. Human judgment, on the other hand, can sometimes capitalize on idiosyncratic features that are difficult or impossible to model.

Human judgment can also result in errors, but models are perfectly consistent; they never get bored, tired, or distracted, as people do. Models are never inconsistent or random—in fact, they may be consistent to a fault. The important question, then, is which method leads to less overall error.

Or to put the question another way, if we accept the inevitability of some error from using a formal model, will we end up with less overall error by using the model rather than human judgment? According to the results of psychological experiments on probability learning, the answer is yes.

In these studies, subjects are asked to predict which of two lights—one red, one green—will go on. If they guess right, the subjects get a cash reward. If they guess wrong, they get no reward. A random process governs which light goes on, but by arrangement, the red light goes on 60% of the time and the green light, 40%. Subjects are not told about the percentages but have the opportunity to learn about them by participating in the experiment.

The result of this kind of experiment is something called probability matching: subjects learn to respond to cues in the same proportion as they occur. In this case, subjects predict red about 60% of the time and green, 40%. And yet they do not come up with the best predictive strategy that will gain the greatest cash reward, because they are unwilling to accept error.

By predicting red 60% of the time and green 40%, subjects can expect to be right a total of 52% of the time: they will be right on the red light 36% of the time and right on the green light 16% of the time.

But what would happen if subjects were willing to predict red, the more likely color, every time? Such a strategy accepts error; it also leads to 60% correct prediction—8% higher than a strategy that seeks the right answer on every guess.

The subjects would make more money if they accepted error and consistently used a simple mathematical model. Most subjects try to predict perfectly, though, and futilely attempt to discern some nonexistent rule or pattern that determines which light will go on. Any similarity between this example and playing the stock market is purely coincidental.

**Models are static.** This criticism is simply not true. Models can and should be updated with new information as it becomes available. Models are now being developed that learn from the outcomes of predicted events. This work, while still in its early stages, suggests models can learn from experience.

As far as human judgment is concerned, it is simply not clear that people do learn from feedback in making predictions. Part of the difficulty in learning occurs when people make predictive judgments to take action. The outcomes provide only ambiguous feedback on the quality of the predictions.

For example, imagine a case in which the president of the United States takes strong measures to counteract a predicted economic slowdown. Now consider the difficulties of learning from the various possible outcomes. Imagine having no recession as an outcome. This could result either from an incorrect prediction and an ineffective action or from an accurate prediction and a highly effective action. Now imagine a recession as an outcome. This could result either from an accurate prediction and an ineffective action or from an inaccurate prediction and a boomerang action that causes the very malady it is intended to prevent. The problem is this: to learn about our predictive ability requires separating the quality of predictions from the effects of actions based on those predictions.

**Models are not worth their cost.** In general, it is impossible to evaluate the argument that any marginal increase in accuracy from using models does not outweigh the extra cost of building them. If a model is used to make enough predictions, however, even small increases in accuracy can produce large benefits.

For example, in the late 1970s, AT&T conducted a study to determine the characteristics of good and bad credit risks.[1] Management incorporated the results in a set of decision rules that it used to determine which new customers should be required to provide deposits. In developing these rules, AT&T went through a time when it granted credit to customers it would have previously classified as both good risks and bad risks. As a result, the rules were validated across the whole range of customer characteristics. By implementing the decision rules, management realized an estimated annual reduction of $137 million in bad debts. While no figures are available on the cost of creating and maintaining the model, it is difficult to believe that the savings did not warrant the expense.

While many phenomena we try to predict are complex, the rules for reasoning forward need not match this complexity. Many successful applications have involved simple combinations of just a few variables. Sometimes the rules develop from modeling an expert's past judgments, sometimes simply by averaging past decisions, and sometimes just by aggregating a few relevant variables.

## Backward and Forward

Our everyday experience is filled with examples of thinking backward and thinking forward. We are constantly using both modes of reasoning, separately and together, and we are constantly confounded in our efforts.

While explicit rules or models are the best tools to use for reasoning forward, intuition or notions of cause can often exert a powerful influence on the predictions we make. When people take actions in situations where random processes produce the outcomes, they are sometimes subject to delusions of control. For instance, people tend to believe that lottery tickets they personally select have a greater chance of winning than those selected for them by a lottery administrator.

By the same token, in complex situations, we may rely too heavily on planning and forecasting and underestimate the importance of random factors in the environment. That reliance can also lead to delusions of control. The best posture is to remain skeptical toward all undocumented claims of predictive accuracy, whether they are derived from experts, models, or both. Remember the seersucker theory of prediction: for every seer, there is a sucker.[2]

An important paper on how to improve predictive ability once expressed the task of thinking forward in this way: "The whole trick is to decide what variables to look at and then know how to add."[3] But "the trick" is a difficult one that requires complex thinking backward. Indeed, computer scientists who are working to build programs that simulate the understanding process by means of artificial intelligence have had great difficulty in modeling this process. A recent example concerns a program they wrote to simulate the comprehension of newspaper headlines. They provided the program with background knowledge and a set of rules to rewrite the headlines. One such headline was: "World shaken. Pope shot." The computer interpreted this as: "Earthquake in Italy. One dead."

Although the psychological study of judgment and decision making has concentrated on separating thinking backward from thinking forward by clarifying the distinction, the two modes of reasoning are interdependent. Like the god Janus in Roman mythology, whose head has two faces, one facing forward, the other backward, our thinking goes in both directions whenever we put our minds to work on making a decision.

# Notes

1. J. L. Showers and L.M. Chakrin, "Reducing Uncollectible Revenue from Residential Telephone Customers," *Interfaces*, December 1981, p. 21.

2. J. Scott Armstrong, *Long-Range Forecasting* (New York: Wiley, 1978).

3. Robyn M. Dawes and Bernard Corrigan, "Linear Models in Decision Making," *Psychological Bulletin*, February 1974, p. 95.

**Originally published in January–February 1987**
**Reprint 87107**

# Disruptive Technologies:

## Catching the Wave

JOSEPH L. BOWER AND

CLAYTON M. CHRISTENSEN

### Executive Summary

ONE OF THE MOST CONSISTENT PATTERNS in business is the failure of leading companies to stay at the
top of their industries when technologies or markets
change. Why is it that established companies invest
aggressively—and successfully—in the technologies necessary to retain their current customers but then fail to
make the technological investments that customers of the
future will demand? The fundamental reason is that leading companies succumb to one of the most popular, and
valuable, management dogmas: they stay close to their
customers.

Customers wield extraordinary power in directing a
company's investments. But what happens when a new
technology emerges that customers reject because it
doesn't address their needs as effectively as a company's
current approach? In an ongoing study of technological

change, the authors found that most established companies are consistently ahead of their industries in developing and commercializing new technologies as long as those technologies address the next-generation-performance needs of their customers, However, an industry's leaders are rarely in the forefront of commercializing new technologies that don't initially meet the functional demands of mainstream customers and appeal only to small or emerging markets.

To remain at the top of their industries, managers must first be able to spot the technologies that fall into this category. To pursue these technologies, managers must protect them from the processes and incentives that are geared to serving mainstream customers. And the only way to do that is to create organizations that are completely independent of the mainstream business.

---

ONE OF THE MOST CONSISTENT PATTERNS IN BUSINESS IS the failure of leading companies to stay at the top of their industries when technologies or markets change. Goodyear and Firestone entered the radial-tire market quite late. Xerox let Canon create the small-copier market. Bucyrus-Erie allowed Caterpillar and Deere to take over the mechanical excavator market. Sears gave way to Wal-Mart.

The pattern of failure has been especially striking in the computer industry. IBM dominated the mainframe market but missed by years the emergence of minicomputers, which were technologically much simpler than mainframes. Digital Equipment dominated the minicomputer market with innovations like its VAX architecture but missed the personal-computer market almost completely. Apple Computer led the world of personal computing and established the standard for user-friendly computing but lagged five years behind the leaders in bringing its portable computer to market.

Why is it that companies like these invest aggressively—and successfully—in the technologies necessary to retain their current customers but then fail to make certain other technological investments that customers of the future will demand? Undoubtedly, bureaucracy, arrogance, tired executive blood, poor planning, and short-term investment horizons have all played a role. But a more fundamental reason lies at the heart of the paradox: leading companies succumb to one of the most popular, and valuable, management dogmas. They stay close to their customers.

Although most managers like to think they are in control, customers wield extraordinary power in directing a company's investments. Before managers decide to launch a technology, develop a product, build a plant, or establish new channels of distribution, they must look to their customers first: Do their customers want it? How big will the market be? Will the investment be profitable? The more astutely managers ask and answer these questions, the more completely their investments will be aligned with the needs of their customers.

This is the way a well-managed company should operate. Right? But what happens when customers reject a new technology, product concept, or way of doing business because it does *not* address their needs as effectively as a company's current approach? The large photocopying centers that represented the core of Xerox's customer base at first had no use for small, slow tabletop copiers. The excavation contractors that had relied on Bucyrus-Erie's big-bucket steam- and diesel-powered cable shovels didn't want hydraulic excavators because initially they were small and weak. IBM's large

*Managers must beware of ignoring new technologies that don't initially meet the needs of their mainstream customers.*

commercial, government, and industrial customers saw no immediate use for minicomputers. In each instance, companies listened to their customers, gave

them the product performance they were looking for, and, in the end, were hurt by the very technologies their customers led them to ignore.

We have seen this pattern repeatedly in an on-going study of leading companies in a variety of industries that have confronted technological change. The research shows that most well-managed, established companies are consistently ahead of their industries in developing and commercializing new technologies—from incremental improvements to radically new approaches—as long as those technologies address the next-generation performance needs of their customers. However, these same companies are rarely in the forefront of commercializing new technologies that don't initially meet the needs of mainstream customers and appeal only to small or emerging markets.

Using the rational, analytical investment processes that most well-managed companies have developed, it is nearly impossible to build a cogent case for diverting resources from known customer needs in established markets to markets and customers that seem insignificant or do not yet exist. After all, meeting the needs of established customers and fending off competitors takes all the resources a company has, and then some. In well-managed companies, the processes used to identify customers' needs, forecast technological trends, assess profitability, allocate resources across competing proposals for investment, and take new products to market are focused—for all the right reasons—on current customers and markets. These processes are designed to weed out proposed products and technologies that do *not* address customers' needs.

In fact, the processes and incentives that companies use to keep focused on their main customers work so well that they blind those companies to important new technologies in emerging markets. Many companies have learned the hard way the perils of ignoring new technologies that do not initially meet the needs of mainstream customers. For example, although personal computers did not meet the requirements of mainstream minicomputer users in the early 1980s, the computing power of the desktop machines improved at a much faster rate than minicomputer users' *demands* for computing power did. As a result, personal computers caught up with the computing needs of many of the customers of Wang, Prime, Nixdorf, Data General, and Digital Equipment. Today they are performance-competitive with minicomputers in many applications. For the minicomputer makers, keeping close to mainstream customers and ignoring what were initially low-performance desktop technologies used by seemingly insignificant customers in emerging markets was a rational decision—but one that proved disastrous.

The technological changes that damage established companies are usually not radically new or difficult from a *technological* point of view. They do, however, have two important characteristics: First, they typically present a different package of performance attributes—ones that, at least at the outset, are not valued by existing customers. Second, the performance attributes that existing customers do value improve at such a rapid rate that the new technology can later invade those established markets. Only at this point will mainstream customers want the technology. Unfortunately for the established suppliers, by then it is often too late: the pioneers of the new technology dominate the market.

It follows, then, that senior executives must first be able to spot the technologies that seem to fall into this category. Next, to commercialize and develop the new technologies, managers must protect them from the processes and incentives that are geared to serving established customers. And the only way to protect them is to create organizations that are completely independent from the mainstream business.

NO INDUSTRY DEMONSTRATES THE DANGER of staying too close to customers more dramatically than the hard-disk-drive industry. Between 1976 and 1992, disk-drive performance improved at a stunning rate: the physical size of a 100-megabyte (MB) system shrank from 5,400 to 8 cubic inches, and the cost per MB fell from $560 to $5. Technological change, of course, drove these breathtaking achievements. About half of the improvement came from a host of radical advances that were critical to continued improvements in disk-drive performance; the other half came from incremental advances.

The pattern in the disk-drive industry has been repeated in many other industries: the leading, established companies have consistently led the industry in developing and adopting new technologies that their customers demanded—even when those technologies required completely different technological competencies and manufacturing capabilities from the ones the companies had. In spite of this aggressive technological posture, no single disk-drive manufacturer has been able to dominate the industry for more than a few years. A series of companies have entered the business and risen to prominence, only to be toppled by newcomers who pursued technologies that at first did not meet the needs of mainstream customers. As a result, not one of the independent disk-drive companies that existed in 1976 survives today.

To explain the differences in the impact of certain kinds of technological innovations on a given industry, the concept of *performance trajectories*—the rate at which the performance of a product has improved, and is expected to improve, over time—can be helpful. Almost every industry has a critical performance trajectory. In mechanical excavators, the critical trajectory is the annual improvement in cubic yards of earth moved per minute. In photocopiers, an important performance trajectory is improvement in number of copies per minute. In disk drives, one crucial measure of performance is storage capacity, which has advanced 50% each year on average for a given size of drive.

Different types of technological innovations affect performance trajectories in different ways. On the one hand, *sustaining* technologies tend to maintain a rate of improvement; that is, they give customers something more or better in the attributes they already value. For example, thin-film components in disk drives, which replaced conventional ferrite heads and oxide disks between 1982 and 1990, enabled information to be recorded more densely on disks. Engineers had been pushing the limits of the performance they could wring from ferrite heads and oxide disks, but the drives employing these technologies seemed to have reached the natural limits of an *S* curve. At that point, new thin-film technologies emerged that restored—or sustained—the historical trajectory of performance improvement.

On the other hand, *disruptive* technologies introduce a very different package of attributes from the one mainstream customers historically value, and they often perform far worse along one or two dimensions that are particularly important to those customers. As a rule, mainstream customers are unwilling to use a disruptive product in applications they know and understand. At first, then, disruptive technologies tend to be used and valued only in new markets or new applications; in fact, they generally make possible the emergence of new markets. For example, Sony's early transistor radios sacrificed sound fidelity but created a market for portable radios by offering a new and different package of attributes—small size, light weight, and portability.

In the history of the hard-disk-drive industry, the leaders stumbled at each point of disruptive technological change: when the diameter of disk drives shrank from the original 14 inches to 8 inches, then to 5.25 inches, and finally to 3.5 inches. Each of these new architectures initially offered the market substantially less storage capacity than the typical user in the established market required. For example, the 8-inch drive offered 20 MB when it was introduced, while the primary market for disk drives at that time—mainframes—required 200 MB on average. Not surprisingly, the leading computer manufacturers rejected the 8-inch architecture at first. As a result, their suppliers, whose mainstream products consisted of 14-inch drives with more than 200 MB of capacity, did not pursue the disruptive products aggressively. The pattern was repeated when the 5.25-inch and 3.5-inch drives emerged: established computer makers rejected the drives as inadequate, and, in turn, their disk-drive suppliers ignored them as well.

But while they offered less storage capacity, the disruptive architectures created other important attributes—internal power supplies and smaller size (8-inch drives); still smaller size and low-cost stepper motors (5.25-inch drives); and ruggedness, light weight, and low-power consumption (3.5-inch drives). From the late 1970s to the mid-1980s, the availability of the three drives made possible the development of new markets for minicomputers, desktop PCs, and portable computers, respectively.

Although the smaller drives represented disruptive technological change, each was technologically straightforward. In fact, there were engineers at many leading companies who championed the new technologies and built working prototypes with bootlegged resources before management gave a formal go-ahead. Still, the leading companies could not move the products through their organizations and into the market in a timely way. Each time a disruptive technology emerged, between one-half and two-thirds of the established manufacturers failed to introduce models employing the new architecture—in stark contrast to their timely launches of critical sustaining technologies. Those companies that finally did launch new models typically lagged behind entrant companies by two years—eons in an industry whose products' life cycles are often two years. Three waves of entrant companies led these revolutions; they first captured the new markets and then dethroned the leading companies in the mainstream markets.

How could technologies that were initially inferior and useful only to new markets eventually threaten leading companies in established markets? Once the disruptive architectures became established in their new markets, sustaining innovations raised each architecture's performance along steep trajectories—so steep that the performance available from each architecture soon satisfied the needs of customers in the established markets. For example, the 5.25-inch drive, whose initial 5 MB of capacity in 1980 was only a fraction of the capacity that the minicomputer market needed, became fully performance-competitive in the minicomputer market by 1986 and in the mainframe market by 1991. (See the graph "How Disk-Drive Performance Met Market Needs.")

A company's revenue and cost structures play a critical role in the way it evaluates proposed technological innovations. Generally, disruptive technologies look financially unattractive to established companies. The potential revenues from the discernible markets are small, and it is often difficult to project how big the markets for the technology will be over the long term. As a result, managers typically conclude that the technology cannot make a meaningful contribution to corporate growth and, therefore, that it is not worth the management effort required to develop it. In addition, established companies have often installed higher cost structures to serve sustaining technologies than those required by disruptive technologies. As a result, managers typically see themselves as having two choices when deciding whether to pursue disruptive technologies. One is to go *downmarket* and accept the lower profit margins of the emerging markets that the disrup-

*None of the established leaders in the disk-drive industry learned from the experiences of those that fell before them.*

tive technologies will initially serve. The other is to go *upmarket* with sustaining technologies and enter market segments whose profit margins are alluringly high. (For example, the margins of IBM's mainframes are still higher than those of PCs). Any rational resource-allocation process in companies serving established markets will choose going upmarket rather than going down.

Managers of companies that have championed disruptive technologies in emerging markets look at the world quite differently. Without the high cost structures

## How Disk-Drive Performance Met Market Needs

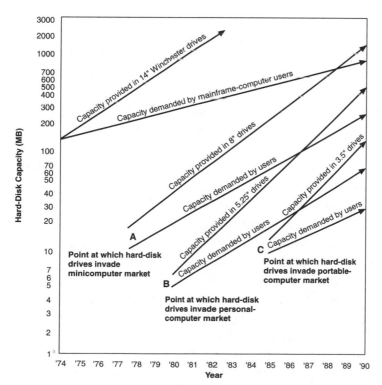

of their established counterparts, these companies find the emerging markets appealing. Once the companies have secured a foothold in the markets and improved the performance of their technologies, the established markets above them, served by high-cost suppliers, look appetizing. When they do attack, the entrant companies find the established players to be easy and unprepared opponents because the opponents have been looking upmarket themselves, discounting the threat from below.

It is tempting to stop at this point and conclude that a valuable lesson has been learned: managers can avoid missing the next wave by paying careful attention to potentially disruptive technologies that do *not* meet current customers' needs. But recognizing the pattern and figuring out how to break it are two different things. Although entrants invaded established markets with new technologies three times in succession, none of the established leaders in the disk-drive industry seemed to learn from the experiences of those that fell before them. Management myopia or lack of foresight cannot explain these failures. The problem is that managers keep doing what has worked in the past: serving the rapidly growing needs of their current customers. The processes that successful, well-managed companies have developed to allocate resources among proposed investments are *incapable* of funneling resources into programs that current customers explicitly don't want and whose profit margins seem unattractive.

Managing the development of new technology is tightly linked to a company's investment processes. Most strategic proposals—to add capacity or to develop new products or processes—take shape at the lower levels of organizations in engineering groups or project

teams. Companies then use analytical planning and bud-
geting systems to select from among the candidates
competing for funds. Proposals to create new businesses
in emerging markets are particularly challenging to
assess because they depend on notoriously unreliable
estimates of market size. Because managers are evaluated on their ability to place the right bets, it is not surprising that in well-managed companies, mid- and top-
level managers back projects in which the market seems
assured. By staying close to lead customers, as they have
been trained to do, managers focus resources on fulfill-
ing the requirements of those reliable customers that
can be served profitably. Risk is reduced—and careers
are safeguarded—by giving known customers what they
want.

SEAGATE TECHNOLOGY'S EXPERIENCE ILLUS-
TRATES THE CONSEQUENCES of relying on such
resource-allocation processes to evaluate disruptive
technologies. By almost any measure, Seagate, based in
Scotts Valley, California, was one of the most successful
and aggressively managed companies in the history of
the microelectronics industry: from its inception in
1980, Seagate's revenues had grown to more than $700
million by 1986. It had pioneered 5.25-inch hard-disk
drives and was the main supplier of them to IBM and
IBM-compatible personal-computer manufacturers. The
company was the leading manufacturer of 5.25-inch
drives at the time the disruptive 3.5-inch drives emerged
in the mid-1980s.

Engineers at Seagate were the second in the industry
to develop working prototypes of 3.5-inch drives. By
early 1985, they had made more than 80 such models

with a low level of company funding. The engineers forwarded the new models to key marketing executives, and the trade press reported that Seagate was actively developing 3.5-inch drives. But Seagate's principal customers—IBM and other manufacturers of AT-class personal computers—showed no interest in the new drives. They wanted to incorporate 40-MB and 60-MB drives in their next-generation models, and Seagate's early 3.5-inch prototypes packed only 10 MB. In response, Seagate's marketing executives lowered their sales forecasts for the new disk drives.

Manufacturing and financial executives at the company pointed out another drawback to the 3.5-inch drives. According to their analysis, the new drives would never be competitive with the 5.25-inch architecture on a cost-per-megabyte basis—an important metric that Seagate's customers used to evaluate disk drives. Given Seagate's cost structure, margins on the higher-capacity 5.25-inch models therefore promised to be much higher than those on the smaller products.

Senior managers quite rationally decided that the 3.5-inch drive would not provide the sales volume and profit margins that Seagate needed from a new product. A former Seagate marketing executive recalled, "We needed a new model that could become the next ST412 [a 5.25-inch drive generating more than $300 million in annual sales, which was nearing the end of its life cycle]. At the time, the entire market for 3.5-inch drives was less than $50 million. The 3.5-inch drive just didn't fit the bill—for sales or profits."

The shelving of the 3.5-inch drive was *not* a signal that Seagate was complacent about innovation. Seagate subsequently introduced new models of 5.25-inch drives at an accelerated rate and, in so doing, introduced an impressive array of sustaining technological improvements, even though introducing them rendered a significant portion of its manufacturing capacity obsolete.

While Seagate's attention was glued to the personal-computer market, former employees of Seagate and other 5.25-inch drive makers, who had become frustrated by their employers' delays in launching 3.5-inch drives, founded a new company, Conner Peripherals. Conner focused on selling its 3.5-inch drives to companies in emerging markets for portable computers and small-footprint desktop products (PCs that take up a smaller amount of space on a desk). Conner's primary customer was Compaq Computer, a customer that Seagate had never served. Seagate's own prosperity, coupled with Conner's focus on customers who valued different disk-drive attributes (ruggedness, physical volume, and weight), minimized the threat Seagate saw in Conner and its 3.5-inch drives.

From its beachhead in the emerging market for portable computers, however, Conner improved the storage capacity of its drives by 50% per year. By the end of 1987, 3.5-inch drives packed the capacity demanded in the mainstream personal-computer market. At this point, Seagate executives took their company's 3.5-inch drive off the shelf, introducing it to the market as a *defensive* response to the attack of entrant companies like Conner and Quantum Corporation, the other pioneer of 3.5-inch drives. But it was too late.

By then, Seagate faced strong competition. For a while, the company was able to defend its existing market by selling 3.5-inch drives to its established customer base—manufacturers and resellers of full-size personal computers. In fact, a large proportion of its 3.5-inch products continued to be shipped in frames that enabled its customers to mount the drives in computers designed to accommodate 5.25-inch drives. But, in the end, Seagate could only struggle to become a second-tier supplier in the new portable-computer market.

In contrast, Conner and Quantum built a dominant position in the new portable-computer market and then used their scale and experience base in designing and manufacturing 3.5-inch products to drive Seagate from the personal-computer market. In their 1994 fiscal years, the combined revenues of Conner and Quantum exceeded $5 billion.

*Seagate paid the price for allowing start-ups to lead the way into emerging markets.*

Seagate's poor timing typifies the responses of many established companies to the emergence of disruptive technologies. Seagate was willing to enter the market for 3.5-inch drives only when it had become large enough to satisfy the company's financial requirements—that is, only when existing customers wanted the new technology. Seagate has survived through its savvy acquisition of Control Data Corporation's disk-drive business in 1990. With CDC's technology base and Seagate's volume-manufacturing expertise, the company has become a powerful player in the business of supplying large-capacity drives for high-end computers. Nonetheless, Seagate has been reduced to a shadow of its former self in the personal-computer market.

IT SHOULD COME AS NO SURPRISE that few companies, when confronted with disruptive technologies, have been able to overcome the handicaps of size or success. But it can be done. There is a method to spotting and cultivating disruptive technologies.

**Determine whether the technology is disruptive or sustaining.** The first step is to decide which of the myriad technologies on the horizon are disruptive and, of those, which are real threats. Most companies have well-conceived processes for identifying and tracking the progress of potentially sustaining technologies, because they are important to serving and protecting current customers. But few have systematic processes in place to identify and track potentially disruptive technologies.

One approach to identifying disruptive technologies is to examine internal disagreements over the development of new products or technologies. Who supports the project and who doesn't? Marketing and financial managers, because of their managerial and financial incentives, will rarely support a disruptive technology. On the other hand, technical personnel with outstanding track records will often persist in arguing that a new market for the technology will emerge—even in the face of opposition from key customers and marketing and financial staff. Disagreement between the two groups often signals a disruptive technology that top-level managers should explore.

**Define the strategic significance of the disruptive technology.** The next step is to ask the right people the right questions about the strategic importance of the disruptive technology. Disruptive technologies tend to stall early in strategic reviews because managers either ask the wrong questions or ask the wrong people the right questions. For example, established companies have regular procedures for asking mainstream customers—especially the important accounts where new ideas are actually tested—to assess the value of innovative products. Generally, these customers are selected because they are the ones striving the hardest to stay ahead of *their* competitors in pushing the performance of *their* products. Hence these customers are most likely to demand the highest performance from their suppliers. For this reason, lead customers are reliably accurate when it comes to assessing the potential of sustaining technologies, but they are reliably *in*accurate when it comes to assessing the potential of disruptive technologies. They are the wrong people to ask.

A simple graph plotting product performance as it is defined in mainstream markets on the vertical axis and time on the horizontal axis can help managers identify both the right questions and the right people to ask. First, draw a line depicting the level of performance and the trajectory of performance improvement that customers have historically enjoyed and are likely to expect in the future. Then locate the estimated initial performance level of the new technology. If the technology is disruptive, the point will lie far below the performance demanded by current customers. (See the graph "How to Assess Disruptive Technologies.")

What is the likely slope of performance improvement of the disruptive technology compared with the slope of performance improvement demanded by existing markets? If knowledgeable technologists believe the new technology might progress faster than the market's demand for performance improvement, then that technology, which does not meet customers' needs today, may very well address them tomorrow. The new technology, therefore, is strategically critical.

Instead of taking this approach, most managers ask the wrong questions. They compare the anticipated rate of performance improvement of the new technology with that of the established technology. If the new technology has the potential to surpass the established one, the reasoning goes, they should get busy developing it.

Pretty simple. But this sort of comparison, while valid for sustaining technologies, misses the central strategic issue in assessing potentially disruptive technologies. Many of the disruptive technologies we studied *never* surpassed the capability of the old technology. It is the trajectory of the disruptive technology compared with that of the *market* that is significant. For example, the reason the mainframe-computer market is shrinking is not that personal computers outperform mainframes but because personal computers networked with a file server meet the computing and data-storage needs of many organizations effectively. Mainframe-computer makers are reeling not because the performance of personal-computing technology surpassed the performance of mainframe *technology* but because it intersected with the performance demanded by the established *market*.

## How to Assess Disruptive Technologies

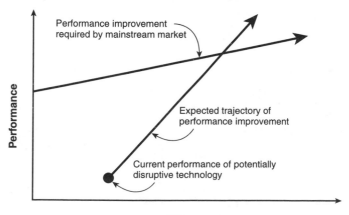

Consider the graph again. If technologists believe that the new technology will progress at the same rate as the market's demand for performance improvement, the disruptive technology may be slower to invade established markets. Recall that Seagate had targeted personal computing, where demand for hard-disk capacity per computer was growing at 30% per year. Because the capacity of 3.5-inch drives improved at a much faster rate, leading 3.5-inch-drive makers were able to force Seagate out of the market. However, two other 5.25-inch-drive makers, Maxtor and Micropolis, had targeted the engineering-workstation market, in which demand for hard-disk capacity was insatiable. In that market, the trajectory of capacity demanded was essentially parallel to the trajectory of capacity improvement that technologists could supply in the 3.5-inch architecture. As a result, entering the 3.5-inch-drive business was strategically less critical for those companies than it was for Seagate.

**Locate the initial market for the disruptive technology.** Once managers have determined that a new technology is disruptive and strategically critical, the next step is to locate the initial markets for that technology. Market research, the tool that managers have traditionally relied on, is seldom helpful: at the point a company needs to make a strategic commitment to a disruptive technology, no concrete market exists. When Edwin Land asked Polaroid's market researchers to assess the potential sales of his new camera, they concluded that Polaroid would sell a mere

*Small, hungry organizations are good at agilely changing product and market strategies.*

100,000 cameras over the product's lifetime; few people they interviewed could imagine the uses of instant photography.

Because disruptive technologies frequently signal the emergence of new markets or market segments, managers must *create* information about such markets— who the customers will be, which dimensions of product performance will matter most to which customers, what the right price points will be. Managers can create this kind of information only by experimenting rapidly, iteratively, and inexpensively with both the product and the market.

For established companies to undertake such experiments is very difficult. The resource-allocation processes that are critical to profitability and competitiveness will not—and should not—direct resources to markets in which sales will be relatively small. How, then, can an established company probe a market for a disruptive technology? Let start-ups—either ones the company funds or others with no connection to the company— conduct the experiments. Small, hungry organizations are good at placing economical bets, rolling with the punches, and agilely changing product and market strategies in response to feedback from initial forays into the market.

Consider Apple Computer in its start-up days. The company's original product, the Apple I, was a flop when it was launched in 1977. But Apple had not placed a huge bet on the product and had gotten at least *something* into the hands of early users quickly. The company learned a lot from the Apple I about the new technology and about what customers wanted and did not want. Just as important, a group of *customers* learned about what they did and did not want from personal computers. Armed with this information, Apple launched the Apple II quite successfully.

Many companies could have learned the same valuable lessons by watching Apple closely. In fact, some companies pursue an explicit strategy of being *second to invent*—allowing small pioneers to lead the way into uncharted market territory. For instance, IBM let Apple, Commodore, and Tandy define the personal computer. It then aggressively entered the market and built a considerable personal-computer business.

But IBM's relative success in entering a new market late is the exception, not the rule. All too often, successful companies hold the performance of small-market pioneers to the financial standards they apply to their own performance. In an attempt to ensure that they are using their resources well, companies explicitly or implicitly set relatively high thresholds for the size of the markets they should consider entering. This approach sentences them to making late entries into markets already filled with powerful players.

For example, when the 3.5-inch drive emerged, Seagate needed a $300-million-a-year product to replace its mature flagship 5.25-inch model, the ST412, and the 3.5-inch market wasn't large enough. Over the next two years, when the trade press asked when Seagate would introduce its 3.5-inch drive, company executives consistently responded that there was no market yet. There actually *was* a market, and it was growing rapidly. The signals that Seagate was picking up about the market, influenced as they were by customers who didn't want 3.5-inch drives, were misleading. When Seagate finally introduced its 3.5-inch drive in 1987, more than $750 million in 3.5-inch drives had already been sold. Information about the market's size had been widely available throughout the industry. But it wasn't compelling enough to shift the focus of Seagate's managers. They continued to look at the new market through the eyes of their current customers and in the context of their current financial structure.

The posture of today's leading disk-drive makers toward the newest disruptive technology, 1.8-inch drives, is eerily familiar. Each of the industry leaders has designed one or more models of the tiny drives, and the models are sitting on shelves. Their capacity is too low to be used in notebook computers, and no one yet knows where the initial market for 1.8-inch drives will be. Fax machines, printers, and automobile dashboard mapping systems are all candidates. "There just isn't a market," complained one industry executive. "We've got the product, and the sales force can take orders for it. But there are no orders because nobody needs it. It just sits there." This executive has not considered the fact that his sales force has no incentive to sell the 1.8-inch drives instead of the higher-margin products it sells to higher-volume customers. And while the 1.8-inch drive is sitting on the shelf at his company and others, last year more than $50 million worth of 1.8-inch drives were sold, almost all by start-ups. This year, the market will be an estimated $150 million.

To avoid allowing small, pioneering companies to dominate new markets, executives must personally monitor the available intelligence on the progress of pioneering companies through monthly meetings with technologists, academics, venture capitalists, and other nontraditional sources of information. They *cannot* rely on the company's traditional channels for gauging markets because those channels were not designed for that purpose.

**Place responsibility for building a disruptive-technology business in an independent organization.**
The strategy of forming small teams into skunk-works projects to isolate them from the stifling demands of mainstream organizations is widely known but poorly understood. For example, isolating a team of engineers so that it can develop a radically new sustaining technology just because that technology is radically different is a fundamental misapplication of the skunk-works approach. Managing out of context is also unnecessary in the unusual event that a disruptive technology is more financially attractive than existing products. Consider Intel's transition from dynamic random access memory (DRAM) chips to microprocessors. Intel's early microprocessor business had a higher gross margin than that of its DRAM business; in other words, Intel's normal resource-allocation process naturally provided the new business with the resources it needed.[1]

Creating a separate organization is necessary only when the disruptive technology has a lower profit margin than the mainstream business and must serve the unique needs of a new set of customers. CDC, for example, successfully created a remote organization to commercialize its 5.25-inch drive. Through 1980, CDC was the dominant independent disk-drive supplier due to its expertise in making 14-inch drives for mainframe-computer makers. When the 8-inch drive emerged, CDC launched a late development effort, but its engineers were repeatedly pulled off the project to solve problems for the more profitable, higher-priority 14-inch projects targeted at the company's most important customers. As a result, CDC was three years late in launching its first 8-inch product and never captured more than 5% of that market.

When the 5.25-inch generation arrived, CDC decided that it would face the new challenge more strategically. The company assigned a small group of engineers and marketers in Oklahoma City, Oklahoma, far from the mainstream organization's customers, the task of developing and commercializing a competitive 5.25-inch product. "We needed to launch it in an environment in which everybody got excited about a $50,000 order," one executive recalled. "In Minneapolis, you needed a $1 million order to turn anyone's head." CDC never regained the 70% share it had once enjoyed in the market for mainframe disk drives, but its Oklahoma City operation secured a profitable 20% of the high-performance 5.25-inch market.

Had Apple created a similar organization to develop its Newton personal digital assistant (PDA), those who have pronounced it a flop might have deemed it a success. In launching the product, Apple made the mistake of acting as if it were dealing with an established market. Apple managers went into the PDA project assuming that it had to make a significant contribution to corporate growth. Accordingly, they researched customer desires exhaustively and then bet huge sums launching the Newton.

*Every company that has tried to manage mainstream and disruptive businesses within a single organization failed.* Had Apple made a more modest technological and financial bet and entrusted the Newton to an organization the size that Apple itself was when it launched the Apple I, the outcome might have been different. The Newton might have been seen more broadly as a solid step forward in the quest to discover what customers really want. In fact, many more Newtons than Apple I models were sold within a year of their introduction.

**Keep the disruptive organization independent.** Established companies can only dominate emerging markets by creating small organizations of the sort CDC created in Oklahoma City. But what should they do when the emerging market becomes large and established?

Most managers assume that once a spin-off has become commercially viable in a new market, it should be integrated into the mainstream organization. They reason that the fixed costs associated with engineering, manufacturing, sales, and distribution activities can be shared across a broader group of customers and products.

*In order that it may live, a corporation must be willing to see business units die.*

This approach might work with sustaining technologies; however, with disruptive technologies, folding the spin-off into the mainstream organization can be disastrous. When the independent and mainstream organizations are folded together in order to share resources, debilitating arguments inevitably arise over which groups get what resources and whether or when to cannibalize established products. In the history of the disk-drive industry, *every* company that has tried to manage mainstream and disruptive businesses within a single organization failed.

No matter the industry, a corporation consists of business units with finite life spans: the technological and market bases of any business will eventually disappear. Disruptive technologies are part of that cycle. Companies that understand this process can create new businesses to replace the ones that must inevitably die. To do so, companies must give managers of disruptive innovation free rein to realize the technology's full potential—even if it means ultimately killing the mainstream business. For the corporation to live, it must be willing to see business units die. If the corporation doesn't kill them off itself, competitors will.

The key to prospering at points of disruptive change is not simply to take more risks, invest for the long term, or fight bureaucracy. The key is to manage strategically important disruptive technologies in an organizational context where small orders create energy, where fast low-cost forays into ill-defined markets are possible, and where overhead is low enough to permit profit even in emerging markets.

Managers of established companies can master disruptive technologies with extraordinary success. But when they seek to develop and launch a disruptive technology that is rejected by important customers within the context of the mainstream business's financial demands, they fail—not because they make the wrong decisions, but because they make the right decisions for circumstances that are about to become history.

# Note

1. Robert A. Burgelman, "Fading Memories: A Process Theory of Strategic Business Exit in Dynamic Environments," *Administrative Science Quarterly 39* (1994), pp. 24–56.

**Originally published in January–February 1995**
**Reprint 95103**

# Time Pacing

## Competing in Markets That Won't Stand Still

KATHLEEN M. EISENHARDT AND

SHONA L. BROWN

## Executive Summary

MOST COMPANIES CHANGE IN REACTION to events such as moves by the competition, shifts in technology, or new customer demands. In fairly stable markets, "event pacing" is an effective way to deal with change. But successful companies in rapidly changing, intensely competitive industries take a different approach. They change proactively, through regular deadlines. The authors call this strategy *time pacing*.

Like a metronome, time pacing creates a rhythm to which managers can synchronize the speed and intensity of their efforts. For example, 3M dictates that 30% of its revenues every year will come from new products. Netscape introduces a new product about every six months, and Intel adds a new fabrication facility to its operations approximately every nine months. Time pacing creates a relentless sense of urgency around meeting deadlines and concentrates people on a common set of goals. Its predictability also provides people with a sense of control in otherwise chaotic markets.

The authors show how companies such as Banc One, Cisco Systems, Dell Computer, Emerson Electric, Gillette, Intel, Netscape, Shiseido, and Sony implement the two essentials of time pacing. The first is managing transitions—the shift, for example, from one new-product-development project to the next. The second is setting the right rhythm for change. Companies that march to the rhythm of time pacing build momentum, and companies that effectively manage transitions sustain that momentum without missing important beats.

---

Back in 1965, GORDON MOORE, a cofounder of Intel Corporation, prophesied that the capacity of the microprocessor computer chip would double every 18 months. Moore's Law, as it has since become known, may sound like a law of physics, but it's not. Instead, it's a business objective that Intel's engineers and managers have taken to heart. Over time, Intel has created a treadmill of new-product introductions that have set a blistering pace in its industry. In the decade between 1987 and 1997, Intel generated an astounding average annual return to investors of 44%. Even more impressive, recently Intel's annual earnings equaled those of the top ten personal computer firms *combined.*

Although few companies will ever enjoy a market position like Intel's, managers can learn a key lesson from the world's premier chip maker. Intel is certainly the most visible—but by no means the only—practitioner of *time pacing*, a strategy for competing in fast-changing, unpredictable markets by scheduling change at predictable time intervals. Not only does Intel make Moore's Law a reality through its new-product introductions, but it also time-paces in other key areas. For example, about every nine months, Intel adds a new fabrication facility to its operations. CEO Andy Grove says, "We build factories two years in advance of needing them, before we have the products to run in them and before we know that the industry is going to grow." By expanding its capacity in this predictable way, Intel deters rivals from entering the business and blocks them from gaining a toehold should Intel be unable to meet demand.

Small and large companies, high and low tech alike, can benefit from time pacing, especially in markets that won't stand still. Cisco Systems, Emerson Electric, Gillette, Netscape, SAP, Sony, Starbucks, and 3M all use time pacing in one form or another. In rapidly shifting industries, time pacing can help managers anticipate change and perhaps, like Intel, set the pace for change. But even in industries in

*Like a metronome, time pacing creates a predictable rhythm for change in a company.*

which the rate of change is less than warp speed, time pacing can counteract the natural tendency of managers to wait too long, move too slowly, and lose momentum.

Our understanding of time pacing emerged from almost a decade of research into the drivers of success in high-velocity, intensely competitive industries. One phase of the research took us inside 12 successful companies in different segments of the computer industry—an industry that serves as a prototype for this new competitive reality. We tested the relevance of these ideas in

other industries as well, through targeted case studies
and consulting work with executives. What we found is
that wherever managers were coping with changing
business environments, time pacing was critical to their
success, helping them resolve the fundamental dilemma
of how often to change.

## Time Pacing Versus Event Pacing

For most managers, *event pacing* constitutes the familiar
and natural order of things. Companies change in
response to events such as moves by the competition,
shifts in technology, poor financial performance, or new
customer demands. Event pacing is about creating a
new product when a promising technology comes out of
the R&D laboratory, entering a new market in response
to a move by a competitor, or making an acquisition because an attractive target becomes available. Managers who event-pace follow a plan and deviate from it only

*3M's dictum that 30% of
revenues must come from
new products every year
lets people gauge what they
need to do and when.*

when performance weakens. In markets that are stable,
event pacing is an opportunistic and effective way to
deal with change. By definition, however, it is also a
reactive and often erratic strategy.

In contrast, time pacing refers to creating new products or services, launching new businesses, or entering
new markets according to the calendar.[1] Even though
time-paced companies can be extraordinarily fast, it is
important not to confuse time pacing with speed. By
definition, time pacing is regular, rhythmic, and proac-
tive. For example, 3M dictates that 30% of revenues will

come from new products every year, Netscape introduces a new product about every six months, British Airways refreshes its service classes every five years, and Starbucks opens 300 stores per year to hit the goal of 2,000 outlets by the year 2000. Time pacing is about running a business through regular deadlines to which managers synchronize the speed and intensity of their efforts. Like a metronome, time pacing creates a predictable rhythm for change in a company.

In the companies we studied, time pacing had a powerful psychological impact. Time pacing creates a relentless sense of urgency around meeting deadlines and concentrates individual and team energy around common goals. As one manager says, "It's like running a marathon in 100-yard bursts." Although the tempo may be fast, it is predictable and so gives people a sense of control in otherwise chaotic markets. People become focused, efficient, and confident about the task at hand, which leads to enhanced performance.

In addition to creating a sense of urgency, time pacing disciplines managers to excel at two critical, but often neglected, processes essential to success in changing markets. The first is managing transitions, or the shifts from one activity to the next. The second is managing rhythm, or the pace at which companies change. Companies that march to the rhythm of time pacing build momentum, and companies that effectively manage transitions sustain that momentum without missing important beats.

## Managing Transitions

Transitions are notoriously complicated, making them a weak link for companies in changing markets. Common transitions include a shift from one product-development project, advertising campaign, or season of merchandise to the next. Other examples include entering or leaving markets, absorbing new acquisitions, launching new alliances, and bringing volume production on-line.

Transitions typically involve a large number of people, many of whom are not used to working with one another. Because transitions occur less frequently than other activities, managers have fewer opportunities to learn from experience. Communication easily breaks down. Missteps often turn into costly delays. In short, Murphy's Law clearly applies in transitions. (See "A Solution for New-Product Development," on page 194.)

Because major transitions are periods when companies are likely to stumble, we expected to find that managers would devote extra attention to them. The surprise is that they don't. They manage the product development process but not the switch from one project to the next. They spend months analyzing an acquisition but far less time planning the integration. Some managers simply ignore transitions, hoping that somehow they will get from one activity to the next.

*In fast-paced markets, transitions are like changing the fan belt while the car is still moving.*

When transitions are poor, businesses lose position, stumble, and fall behind. Blockbuster Video is a recent casualty of poor transition management. In an attempt to cut costs, Blockbuster decided to bring its distribution of videos in-house. But Blockbuster made the mistake of switching from its third-party distributor to its own newly designed, automated facility in Texas before its new system was up and running—and the company has been playing catch-up ever since. The snafu has caused repeated delays in getting the latest videos from the warehouse to Blockbuster's local stores, dealing a blow to the company's performance. In 1997, cash flow dropped a precipitous 70%.

In contrast, companies that manage by time pacing learn to choreograph important transitions—and to shorten the time it takes to execute them. Gillette, for example, smoothly executes about 20 new-product transitions per year. Like a pharmaceuticals company, Gillette sees itself as managing a steady flow of products—developing, launching, and harvesting products all at the same time. Gillette manages this balanced product pipeline through a disciplined transition process. It does not release a product prototype into volume production until a mock-up of the next product to follow is available. The wildly successful Sensor razor, for example, was not launched until its successor product, Excel, was in development. In turn, Excel was not launched until its successor product and more than ten candidate products after that were under development. CEO Al Zeien describes Gillette's strategy as "not just reacting to competitors" but as "orchestrating and commanding a business."

Beyond choreographing its transitions, Gillette has worked to slash the time it takes to execute them. After launching the Sensor line in the domestic market, it took Gillette four years to penetrate all of its markets. With its successor line, Excel, Gillette was able to cut that time to three years. Not only does this hasten the company's revenue flow, but it also prevents competitors from copying Gillette's products in one market and introducing them into another before Gillette does.

Gillette has also focused its attention on developing an effective transition process for entering new geographic markets. The company uses its most popular product—razor blades—to establish a beachhead in new countries. During this initial entry, Gillette builds its distribution infrastructure; operating margins are often small and the company may actually lose money. But as other products, such as hair care appliances and toothbrushes, start to fill the warehouses and flow to retailers, Gillette's costs drop and profits rise. These transitions into new markets have been further refined, with variations in the process depending on the level of development in the country. The result is that Gillette consistently hits its target of 40% of sales from new products, a remarkable feat for a consumer-packaged-goods company.

## WHERE TRANSITIONS MATTER MOST

Although transitions are always important, they are especially so in fast-changing markets where, as one manager put it, "transitions are like changing the fan belt while the car is still moving." When the pace is fast, there are simply more transitions, and so they command a larger share of managers' time. Moreover, the transitions themselves are more critical because the faster the market is moving, the harder it is to catch up once you stumble. It's like competing in the 4 × 100 meter relay—the laps are so short that the execution of the baton passes often determines the outcome of the race.

Consider Netscape. To meet its key challenge of running faster than Microsoft and IBM's Lotus, it has shortened transitions of all types. Before Netscape, other companies in the industry typically paced themselves in 12-month product-development cycles, which were followed by beta site testing and then product shipment. Then Netscape streamlined its approach to product launches. The company slashed product intervals (technical guru, Marc Andreessen, wanted three months but settled for six), effectively doubling the number of transitions needed and so upping the ante on executing transitions well. It then shortened the transitions by forgoing the standard practice of using a few major beta test sites. It simply released prototype products onto the Internet and waited for users to give them feedback on problem areas. Suddenly, Netscape had an army of debuggers who could quickly refine its prototype into a finished product—which the company was then able to launch, often for free, on the Web. This fast and smooth transition process helped Netscape maintain its technical lead in browsers.

*Executing transitions in rapidly changing markets is like running the 4 × 100 relay—the laps are so short that the baton passes often determine the outcome of the race.*

Effective management of transitions is often critical to companies in markets characterized by constantly shifting opportunities. One global computing company that we studied—we'll call it Andromeda—has a particularly effective process for entering new markets. An executive at the group level is responsible for matching new opportunities with existing businesses. When this executive identifies a new market opportunity or when one bubbles up from below, the transition process begins. In the first month, the group executive develops three or four alternative homes, either in existing divisions or as a new stand-alone venture. The alternative venues are compared according to how well they fit with the opportunity in terms of their technology, markets, manufacturing, and distribution. But Andromeda's managers also consider which of its divisions needs a fresh opportunity to kick-start growth. The choice is made quickly—and within four months from the start of the transition process, resources are formally allocated to the new business, and the top management team is put in place. At that four-month mark, the clock starts ticking, and the team has two years to hit key performance metrics for revenue and profits.

Contrast Andromeda's choreographed process for entering new markets with what we observed at a comparable company we'll call Buccaneer. There managers identified a promising multimedia opportunity but did not have a formal way to enter new markets. Because each opportunity was treated as a unique event, this one required idiosyncratic thinking about whether and how to proceed. Managers needed eight months to "resource" the opportunity. In the interim, three competitors entered the market, preempting Buccaneer and demoralizing the team that had worked on the project.

For companies that attempt to grow quickly through acquisitions, the postmerger integration process is a critical transition. Consider Banc One, a market leader among superregional banks. For a number of years, Banc One bought smaller banks at a measured pace of about ten acquisitions per year, with four to six acquisitions occurring at any one time. The transition process often began on the day that the merger was announced: all employees received a videotape welcoming them to Banc One and explaining what the new affiliation would mean. A team of about 30 Banc One staffers then quickly began a complex process made up of simultaneous activities conducted along multiple fronts. For example, the marketing and retailing departments mapped the affiliate's products onto Banc One's portfolio while the electronic banking department assessed ATM volume. Banc One also assigned the new bank a comparable "mentor" institution that had recently undergone a similar conversion, providing a model for the acquiree of what a postconversion operation should look like. After a 180-day transition process, the final changeover occurred on a single weekend. The old systems were shut down on Friday, and the Banc One system was running on Monday. This choreographed process enabled Banc One to fold in acquisitions quickly and thus move rapidly into the ranks of the largest and most successful U.S. banks.[2]

## THE BEST TRANSITIONS

The best transitions do more than simply take a company from point A to point B. Managers can actually use these transitions to learn, reflect, change direction, and accomplish other goals. Andromeda's process for entering new markets doesn't just let the company deploy resources quickly in order to capture opportunities. It also allows the company to achieve other objectives, such as boosting the performance of flagging operating units. Similarly, while Banc One is integrating its acquisitions, it also exploits the opportunity to skim off new best practices from the acquired banks, which then can be used throughout the Banc One network. The most successful companies use transitions as opportunities for broader-based change.

But the best transitions have little else in common. Our research showed that specific transition processes varied from company to company. In fact, they were surprisingly arbitrary. What made the difference in companies that effectively managed transitions was that they all had clear, choreographed processes that their employees understood. That point became apparent

when we did a study of product development at two
leading computer companies. Their processes for managing the transition between development projects dif-
fered in almost every significant design aspect. In the
first company, the transition from one project to the
next was led by its technical gurus; in the second, it was
led by the marketing managers. One transition took a
month; the other took three. Each company had a different set of steps, different timing, different specifications
about who should be involved and when. But both transition processes worked because in each case everyone
followed a script.

## Managing Rhythms

If transitions sustain an organization's momentum, the
rhythms that managers set create that momentum.
Rhythm helps people plan ahead and synchronize their
activities. The 3M dictum, for example, that 30% of its
revenues must come from new products every year lets
people gauge what they need to do and when they need
to do it.

Without rhythm, managers tend to be reactive and to
see change as an unwelcome surprise. Yet most pay little
conscious attention to rhythm. Consider, for example,
how many companies are locked into the ritual of
annual planning cycles regardless of the actual pace
their businesses require for success. A critical dimension
of time pacing is setting the right rhythms for change
and synchronizing those rhythms both with the marketplace and with the organization's internal capabilities.
(See "Time-Pacing Basics," on page 196.)

**Get in step with the market.** What is the right
rhythm? The companies we studied that used time pac-

ing effectively were aligned with important rhythms in
the marketplace—such as seasons, suppliers' product
development cycles, or swings in customer spending.
Surprisingly, we found that although these external
rhythms often seemed obvious, their strategic potential
was frequently unrecognized by competitors.

Consider one cold-beverage business we studied—
we'll call it ThirstCo—for which summer is the peak
buying season. ThirstCo decided to exploit this seasonal-
ity by creating a rhythm of new-product introductions
to coincide with the peak in demand. In retrospect, that
seemed like an obvious strategy. But it wasn't at the
time, because the standard practice in the industry was
to introduce new flavors when they came out of the
kitchen, whatever month that happened to be.

In order to execute its rhythm, ThirstCo developed a
choreographed process to make the transition to its new
products. Now each spring, the company begins by test
marketing three or four new flavors, a process that takes
about two months. Managers then select the one or two
most promising offerings in time for a June product
launch. There is even a standard pattern for the launch,
with each new product accompanied by a lottery-type
promotional game.

A more complex example of setting the right rhythm
comes from a large household-goods manufacturer.
Managers at this company had traditionally launched
new products when they were ready. But the company's
key customers, retail giants such as Wal-Mart and Target, relied on regular, seasonal shelf-planning cycles that
varied by category (such as school supplies and small
housewares). By matching its own product-launch cycles
to the retailers' shelf-planning cycles, the manufacturer
was able to win more shelf space and thus more sales.
Why? Because its newest products and the advertising

dollars that accompanied their launch were available when the retailers were replanning their shelf space. Everyone benefited. The retailers were able to stock the latest and most well-promoted products, consumers were delighted to find products they had just seen advertised, and the manufacturer enjoyed an increase in sales.

Even in seemingly chaotic and volatile markets, there are natural rhythms that can set the tempo for time pacing. One midtier computer company was looking for a way to become a leader in the industry and found the answer in time pacing. As personal computer customers were growing more sophisticated, they were relying more heavily on product reviews from computer magazines, such as those regularly published in *PC World.* So the computer company adjusted its product development cycle to match the length of time between reviews and then synchronized its product releases to come out just before the reviews. The result? Magazine editors wrote about the company's latest and most exciting products, giving them an advantage over competitors' older products. The company then used the favorable magazine reviews in its ad campaigns to give its new-product launches an extra boost.

Whereas customers may be the most important source of rhythm for a company, external rhythms from suppliers and complementers are also key. Intel's time-pacing strategy, after all, depends on the company's ability not only to execute its rhythm but also to synchronize with others. If the company pumps out chips that are too fast for the complementary products that work with the chips or if it designs chips for which there aren't enough uses, then Intel falters. So to stay in rhythm, Intel must create "new uses and new users"— which is, in fact, the company's slogan for keeping the market in sync with its own pace. Intel executives now show up in Hollywood, strike deals with video game companies, and are almost anywhere that computing power is in demand.

Intel must also ensure that complementers such as software developers and important customers such as personal computer manufacturers are able to keep up with its pace. To that end, Intel gives developers at these companies early access to its new products. And when its technology sprints ahead of the market and threatens the established rhythm, its engineers step in to find solutions, as they did when the speed of Intel's microprocessors outstripped the technology for accessing data from networks. After all,

*For most companies, getting in step with the market means moving faster. But for some, finding the right rhythm means slowing down.*

who would want Intel's fast multimedia processing chips if it took too long to download data from the Internet? So the company moved into the network interface market in 1991 with interface cards. By enhancing the technology and increasing manufacturing efficiency, Intel was able to improve the product, slash prices by about 40%, and create demand for cheap, fast PC access to networks—and for Intel microprocessors.

For most companies, getting in step with the market means moving faster. Sometimes, however, finding the right rhythm means slowing down, as one chip maker we'll call SiliCo discovered. The performance of some types of semiconductors is primarily driven by the expensive equipment used to make the chips, especially as chip geometries shrink. Suppliers of this equipment tend to operate on two-year development cycles, a cycle twice as long as SiliCo's. By slowing its rate of new-product introductions to match the pace of a key equipment supplier, SiliCo introduced *fewer* products, but each new chip represented a more significant performance advance because it was better designed to leverage the latest equipment from the supplier. By slowing its pace, SiliCo cut its development costs and increased its average revenue per product.

**General management has its rhythms, too.** Time pacing plays a subtle and almost always overlooked role in the general management of any organization. Most managers work around the annual planning-and-review cycle, without questioning whether that's the right interval. But at a major diversified company, managers altered their planning and review process from the traditional annual cycle to one more tailored to the rate of change in specific markets. In businesses like electronic components in which product development time and product life cycles were short, senior executives went to a six-month review cycle. For lines of business such as home appliances in which product life cycles were between one and three years, they stayed with an annual review. For businesses with longer cycles such as heavy industrial equipment, strategic reviews were set for 18 months. These new review periods made more strategic sense. Moreover, the company was able to exploit these changes by having executives from other businesses within the company attend the reviews and influence strategies, particularly around cross-business collaboration opportunities.

In fast-moving segments of the computing and networking industries, the pace is set by executives who manage their companies on incredibly short cycles using real-time information. In the early days of Sun Microsystems, for example, executives monitored the company's performance on a daily basis. The $6 billion networking giant, Cisco Systems, is managed on a fast-time scale as well. Cisco executives watch sales on a weekly basis, a pace that has been impossible for competitors such as Bay Networks to match. The pace at Dell Computer has been termed "Dell-ocity," a waggish takeoff on the company's focus on speed and timing. The result is no joke for Dell's competitors. As CEO Michael Dell says, his company is "setting the pace for the industry." Companies like Dell and Cisco often deliberately choose a pace that competitors cannot sustain. A number of computing and networking companies are looking to enter the telecommunications business because they believe that their speed will give them a decisive competitive advantage over the industry's incumbents.

**Choose a manageable pace.** Companies can only time-pace as fast as their internal capabilities will allow them to move. After all, time pacing requires not just setting a rhythm but also executing it. How many times has a promising business concept been grounded by an unsustainable pace—for instance, when a national roll-out of restaurant outlets exceeds the company's ability to find and train store managers? Companies that time-pace effectively are careful to peg their rhythm to the realities of their internal capabilities. And when that pace falls short of management's ambitions, such companies will ramp up their capabilities.

A fairly simple illustration of how this works is how a credit card company targeted graduating college seniors as customers. The company's managers realized that the optimal time to send direct mail advertising to students was the very brief window between job offers and graduation. If students had job offers in hand, they could be readily evaluated for their financial prospects. And until graduation, the students could easily be reached at their campus addresses. The credit card company decided to execute its direct mail campaign and related card-application processing within this narrow time frame, but doing so required changes in staffing to handle the annual peak work flow.

The principle of matching rhythm to capabilities was the same at Emerson Electric, although the company faced a far more challenging situation. To meet long-term goals for sales growth, Emerson's executives set a target of earning 35% of revenue from the sales of new products—a goal that was initially unreachable because Emerson lacked adequate product-development capacity. So it began a multipronged approach to work up to the rhythm that it had set for itself. It began by streamlining the product development process, cutting development cycle time by about 20%. Simultaneously, it strengthened the marketing staff to increase its understanding of what customers wanted—Emerson could no longer rely so heavily on engineering input. A third move was to cut the size of the active product-development portfolio. Managers believed there were too many products under development, or as they put it, "too many cars on the highway," and no clear sense of priorities. The process of upgrading capabilities took several years, but it enabled Emerson to improve its percentage of sales from new products from 21% in 1991 to more than 30% in recent years, and to extend its enviable record of 40 years of earnings-per-share growth.

## Changing Often Enough

Most of what we've described about time pacing comes from observations of companies that practice it—and from companies that don't. In our work in fast-changing markets, we often see that time pacing helps managers avert the danger of changing too infrequently. By setting a regular pace for change, managers avoid becoming locked into old patterns and habits.

There is also interesting academic work that highlights another common syndrome we have observed—changing too frequently. Computer simulations done by Anjali Sastry of the University of Michigan, for example, show this happening to event-driven players when their environments begin to speed up. Sastry's simulations are programmed with feedback loops and delays: an event takes place, the organization responds by acting, it then gets feedback from the market to which it again may react, and so on. When the simulation mimics a relatively slow market, event pacing works well because it gives managers the time to build competencies that fit the environment.[3] But speed up the rate of change, and event pacing loses its viability. What happens in the simulation is that the organization starts changing *all* the time. It reacts too quickly and never learns to be good at anything.

This research and our own field observations suggest that time pacing can help organizations resist the extreme of changing too often. In rapidly changing, intensely competitive industries, the dilemma of how often to change is acute because the signals for when to change typically are unclear. Does a down month for product sales mean that interest is waning, or is it just a temporary lull? Does a failed initial foray into a market mean that another try will not be successful? If managers change with every signal, then they fail to accomplish tasks and send confusing messages to customers and employees. But if managers don't change, they run the risk of waiting too long and falling too far behind to catch up. Appropriate time pacing helps resolve this dilemma.

Recall Andromeda, the global computing company with the streamlined process for moving into new business opportunities. When Andromeda funds a new venture, it requires managers to stick with that venture until an evaluation point at two years. The trial period cannot be cut short. General Electric's Jack Welch describes a similar discipline at GE surrounding organizational changes that just "needed to sit there—like popcorn kernels in a warm pan." It was only later that "suddenly things began to pop." Thus time pacing helps ensure that managers persist long enough to avoid overreacting to the "noise" that accompanies most new ventures. It balances the perseverance necessary to overcome obstacles along the way with the change that is required when a course of action is failing—a balance that is especially challenging to achieve in rapidly changing markets.

There will always be a place for event pacing in any business that has to cope with inevitable surprises in the marketplace. And although time pacing is not the answer for every business, most companies—especially those in fast-changing markets—cannot afford to ignore it as part of their strategic arsenal. With time pacing, managers can avoid being left behind, gain ground by exploiting rhythms and transitions, and even set the pace of competition. (See "Keeping Up, Gaining Ground, and Setting the Pace," on page 199.)

---

# A Solution for New-Product Development

NEW-PRODUCT DEVELOPMENT is one of the most significant processes for competing in new or shifting markets.

In our research on the computer industry, we observed that time pacing had a direct impact on the timeliness and effectiveness of new products. In companies that time-paced new-product development, transitions between projects were fluid and efficient, and products were typically released on schedule. But in companies that let each project unfold according to its own schedule, the development process was often erratic, inefficient, and riddled with delays.

One major computer company we'll call ComputeCo demonstrated all the pitfalls of managing development without time pacing. At ComputeCo, projects started and ended at unpredictable intervals. Schedules varied from project to project, and they often had to be adjusted when specifications were changed to add new product features. As a result, most projects took longer than planned, although some actually ended earlier.

As old projects wound down, developers attempted to land new project assignments on their own. ComputeCo's developers referred to this inefficient transition between projects as "shopping in the parking lot." As one developer said, the transitions were periods to "hang out with anybody else who is in between projects, to see what's happening, and to wait for something to be lined up."

The beginning of new projects was as haphazard and unpredictable as the completion of old ones. When new projects began, they were assigned to whoever happened to be free, with little thought about whether these were the best people for the job. The result was that development expertise was rarely matched to a project's technical needs.

The unexpected beginnings and endings of projects also created delays because not enough people were available to begin new projects. One manager complained, "I have absolutely no way to staff this project, and I have to figure out how to staff it." Caught between a rock and a hard place, her project was eventually late. We also observed instances at ComputeCo when too many developers were free, and so projects were created simply to make work. Describing one such project, a frustrated manager told us, "This project is not a strategic fit. I would rather put our resources into doing something for the business." The further irony was that when critical projects arose without warning, resources could not be freed up fast enough because they were tied up in make-work projects.

---

# Time-Pacing Basics

THE FOLLOWING THREE SETS of questions can help managers put in place the fundamentals of time pacing in their organizations. The questions focus on developing time-based performance metrics, identifying critical transitions that need to be choreographed, and finding rhythms by looking externally.

1. **Performance Metrics.** Most companies use performance measures that focus on costs, profit, or innovation. Do your current performance metrics also include measures based on time, such as elapsed time, speed, and rate? In product development, for example, consider measures such as the number of products launched per quarter, the average time from concept to commercial launch, and the average downtime between projects. In integrating acquisitions, consider tracking the time until the new organizational structure is finalized, the time it takes for the sales growth rate to turn positive after the acquisition, and

the number of acquisitions absorbed per year. Every critical transition process should be tracked with at least some time-based measures.

2. **Transitions.** Review the critical transitions in your business. Among the most important are shifting from one product-development project to the next, changing merchandise according to the season, entering new markets, absorbing acquisitions, ramping up to volume production, or launching new strategic alliances. Do you have formal processes for managing each critical transition? Can you simplify or shorten them? Can you accomplish more within a transition than simply getting from A to B?

3. **Rhythms.** List your company's own rhythms, and ask yourself which are really attuned to your business and which are merely habit. Are there important areas with no rhythms at all? For each of your key external relationships with buyers, complementers, suppliers, and competitors—list the major rhythms driving their businesses. Would getting in sync with any of those rhythms create new opportunities for you? What would it take for your organization to exploit those opportunities?

---

# Modularity's Role in Keeping the Pace

WHEN FORCED TO MAKE a decision about whether to stay, for example, on schedule or meet a product's feature specifications, companies that time-pace by definition choose to stick with a schedule. The essential, but often overlooked, tool that allows them to do so is modularity.

Consider Sony's Walkman, one of the most successful consumer products of all time. The modularity of

Walkman's design enables Sony to set the pace in its category with a steady stream of on-time product launches. Based on how different customer groups use the product, Sony designed six basic platforms for the Walkman: playback only, playback and record, playback and tuner, professional playback, professional playback and record, and sports. Then, using standard design elements such as color and styling and distinct components such as batteries, Sony added an assortment of features and technical innovations to the basic platforms with relative ease.

In doing so, Sony made both the actual product design and the process itself modular. The result was that, depending on the time constraints created by the competitive dynamics in a particular segment, the company could choose between a faster but partial redesign or a slower but complete redesign.[4]

Modularity is also an important feature of Microsoft's new-product-development process. Although Microsoft is notorious for delays in its operating systems, applications are another story. Here developers design product features as modules and then prioritize them. Because of this modularity, Microsoft can meet release deadlines for products that incorporate the most critical features and roll over those features that are a lower priority to the next time-paced interval.

Modularity is not the province of technology-based companies alone. Consider Japan's 100-year-old Shiseido, now the world's fourth-largest cosmetic company. Japanese consumers are particularly demanding when it comes to refreshed products, sometimes expecting updated offerings as frequently as every month. As Shiseido's president Akira Gemma says, "We see our customers as our own competitors. We need to move ahead not because other brands are doing so but because our customers' needs are changing." Managers at Shiseido modularize their products by separating the development of the products themselves—the shampoos, conditioners, and fragrances—from the packaging. They can then satisfy changing customer demands by refreshing the packaging—by changing the shapes, sizes, and colors of the bottles. They typically change the packaging more often than they change the products themselves.

# Keeping Up, Gaining Ground, and Setting the Pace

TIME PACING OPENS up strategic options for the companies that use it. They can exploit time pacing to gain competitive ground or even to set the pace of competition in an industry.

## Keeping up

In the mid-1990s, computer giant Compaq failed to keep up with the pace of change in several of its key markets. In laptops, for example, Compaq lost its rhythm of new-product introductions when it ran into delays for exotic components. Rival Toshiba sprinted by to capture the number-one position in global market share. Even worse, Compaq failed to keep pace with Intel's transition from its 486 microprocessor architecture to the Pentium processor in its corporate desktop and home models. Compaq again lost ground to PC rivals Dell and Gateway.

Since then, Compaq has gotten back in step. It now synchronizes with Intel's developments in microprocessor technology. And to minimize the risk of losing its pace again, Compaq steers clear of unusual components that are subject to erratic supply.

## Gaining ground

Beyond simply keeping up, companies can use time pacing to gain competitive ground by fully exploiting rhythms and transitions. Consider defense contractor TRW. For its space and defense businesses in the early 1990s, TRW used an annual January-to-January business-planning cycle to budget all its projects in the coming year. But because TRW's prime customer, the U.S. government, was on an October-to-October fiscal year, it was only in the fall that TRW had an accurate picture of all the jobs that the government was putting out to bid. TRW dealt with this uncertainty by setting aside a "reserve" budget in January. Then in October, it used this reserve to bid on contracts that it hadn't anticipated in January.

Simply by changing its planning calendar to match the government's, TRW found it was able to bid on and win more contracts. Instead of holding money in reserve for opportunities that might or might not materialize, TRW could now allocate its entire budget in a more strategic way, placing bets where they were most likely to win. Thus TRW was able to use time pacing to gain ground.

## Setting the pace

Since the inception of the Walkman in 1979, Sony has used time pacing to set the pace of both innovation and market segmentation. Most key technical innovations for this product category—in tape drive mechanisms, batteries, and headphones—came from Sony at a pace of one per year. At the same time, with a slavish dedication to meeting launch dates, Sony drove the market with a pace set at 20 new models per year. (For more about how companies achieve this rhythm, see the insert "Modularity's Role in Keeping the Pace," on page 197.)

The consumer electronics giant also tailored its pacing to particular markets. In Japan, where Sony faced its strongest competition, the company maintained a rapid pace of new-product introductions. Where Sony dominated a particular product category, such as in children's or sports models—it used a slower pace of change. By tailoring its pacing to the competitiveness of its markets, Sony dominates through its model variety even though its average rate of model change was lower than that of the competition. And Sony kept models in the marketplace on average longer than its competitors did.

Sony's ability to set the pace for its industry depended in part on its mastery of critical transitions. Sony was able, for example, to launch products such as the Walkman 2 simultaneously in Europe, Japan, and the United States, preventing competitors from copying the product in one geographic market and from beating Sony to another market with those copycat products.

# Notes

1. For related research on time pacing versus event pacing, see Connie J.G. Gersick, "Pacing Strategic Change: The Case of a New Venture," *Academy of Management Journal*, vol. 37, pp. 9–45.
2. See Gabriel Szulanski, "Appropriability and the Challenge of Scope: Banc One Routinizes Replication," working paper (Wharton School, University of Pennsylvania, 1997).

3. See M. Anjali Sastry, "Problems and Paradoxes in a Model of Punctuated and Organizational Change," *Administrative Science Quarterly*, vol. 42, no. 2, June 1997, pp. 237–275.

4. See Susan Sanderson and Mustafa Uzumeri, "Managing Product Families: The Case of the Sony Walkman," *Research Policy*, vol. 24, 1995.

Originally published in March–April 1998
Reprint 98202

# About the Contributors

JOSEPH L. BOWER is the Donald K. David Professor of Business Administration at the Harvard Business School. He has devoted his research and teaching to the strategic, organizational, and human problems of top management dealing with the rapidly changing global economy. His numerous publications include prizewinning books, articles, and cases. Currently his research focus is "Corporate Value Added," a study of the role played by the corporate office in building multibusiness firms.

ADAM M. BRANDENBURGER is a professor at the Harvard Business School. His research is in the areas of game theory and business strategy. He is the author and coauthor of numerous academic articles on game theory, as well as the coauthor, with Barry J. Nalebuff, of *Co-opetition*, a book applying game theory to management.

SHONA L. BROWN is a consultant with McKinsey & Company, where her work spans multiple technology-based and consumer-focused industries. Dr. Brown's expertise is in the management of innovation, strategy, and marketing in highly uncertain, rapidly changing markets. She is the coauthor, with Kathleen M. Eisenhardt, of *Competing on the Edge: Strategy as Structured Chaos* (HBS Press, 1998).

CLAYTON M. CHRISTENSEN is a professor of business administration at the Harvard Business School, with a joint appointment in the Technology and Operations Management and General Management faculty groups. His research and teaching interests center on the management of technological innovation, developing organizational capabilities, and finding new markets for new technologies. Before joining the Harvard Business School faculty, Dr. Christensen served as chairman and president of CPS Corporation, a firm he cofounded with several MIT professors in 1984 which is now a publicly traded company. His writings have won several awards including the Production and Operations Management Society's 1991 William Abernathy Award, presented to the author of the best paper in the management of technology; the Newcomen Society's award for the best paper in business history in 1993; the 1995 McKinsey Award for the best article published in the *Harvard Business Review;* and the Global Business Book Award for the best business book published in 1997 as well as the Financial Times/Booz · Allen and Hamilton Award for Best Business Book of 1997, both for his book, *The Innovator's Dilemma* (HBS Press, 1997).

HUGH COURTNEY is a management consultant in McKinsey & Company's Washington, D.C., office. One of the leaders of McKinsey's Strategy Practice, he has served clients on a broad range of strategic issues in the chemicals, health care, energy, and telecommunications industries. His current client service and research interests focus on strategy development under uncertainty and applied game theory. Dr. Courtney was an academic economist before joining McKinsey.

HILLEL J. EINHORN was the Wallace W. Booth Professor of Behavioral Science at the University of Chicago Graduate School of Business and the founder and former director of its Center for Decision Research.

KATHLEEN M. EISENHARDT is a professor of strategy and organization in the School of Engineering, Stanford University, and associate director of the Stanford Computer Industry Project. Her research and teaching focus on managing in high-velocity, intensely competitive markets. Her awards include the Pacific Telesis Foundation for her ideas on fast strategic decision making and the Whittemore Prize for her writing on organizing global firms in rapidly changing markets. Professor Eisenhardt has written numerous articles and is the coauthor, with Shona L. Brown, of *Competing on the Edge: Strategy as Structured Chaos* (HBS Press, 1998).

ARIE P. DE GEUS worked for the Royal Dutch/Shell Group for 38 years. Since his retirement, he has advised many government and private institutions and has lectured throughout the world, as well as accepting appointments as visiting fellow at London Business School and as a board member of both the Organizational Learning Center at MIT and the Nijenrode Learning Center in The Netherlands. His publications include an influential article entitled "Planning as Learning" in the *Harvard Business Review*, a lecture entitled "Companies, What Are They?" published by the Royal Society of Arts, London (1995), and the bestselling business book *The Living Company* (HBS Press, 1997), which received the Edwin G. Booz Prize for the most innovative, insightful management book published in 1997.

GARY HAMEL is the founder and chairman of Strategos, a company dedicated to helping its clients get to the future first. He is the Thomas S. Murphy Distinguished Research Fellow at the Harvard Business School as well as a visiting professor of strategic and international management at London Business School. Called "the world's reigning strategy guru" by the *Economist*, Professor Hamel has originated such concepts as strategic intent, core competence, corporate imagination, strategic architecture, and industry foresight. With C.K. Prahalad, he has authored *Competing for the Future* (HBS Press, 1994), hailed by numerous business journals as one of the decade's most influential business books, and has written several articles for *Harvard Business Review*.

ROBIN M. HOGARTH is the Wallace W. Booth Professor of Behavioral Science at the University of Chicago Graduate School of Business. A member of the faculty at Chicago since 1979, he has also served on the faculties of INSEAD and the London Business School. At Chicago, Professor Hogarth directed the Center for Decision Research from 1983 to 1993 and was deputy dean from 1993 to 1998. He has published several books and numerous articles on topics related to decision making and has acted as a consultant to leading international corporations.

JANE KIRKLAND is director of knowledge management at McKinsey & Company. She is responsible for the firm's knowledge management technology and its global research and information services organization; she also has oversight of knowledge management professionals who reside in industry or functional practices. Previously she was a principal in the Cleveland/Pittsburgh Office of McKinsey, where she served clients in the financial services and electronics industries. Her work with these clients focused primarily on strategy.

IAN C. MACMILLAN is the executive director of the Wharton Entrepreneurial Programs, which consist of the Snider Entrepreneurial Research Center and the Goergen Entrepreneurial Management Programs. He is also the George W. Taylor Professor of Entrepreneurial Studies. Dr. MacMillan's articles have appeared in the *Harvard Business Review, Sloan Management Review, Journal of Business Venturing*, and other journals.

RITA GUNTHER MCGRATH is an assistant professor in the management of organizations division at Columbia Business School. Her research focuses on new ventures, entrepreneurship, and technological innovation and has been widely published in both premier academic journals and leading practitioner-oriented journals such as the *Harvard Business Review*. Prior to joining academia, she was a senior information technology manager and consultant. Dr. McGrath currently teaches in the MBA and executive programs at Columbia and works internationally with a wide variety of organizations facing significant strategic challenges.

BARRY J. NALEBUFF is the Milton Steinbach Professor of Economics and Management at Yale University. An expert on game theory, he has written extensively on its applications for managers. He is the coauthor of *Thinking Strategically: The Competitive Edge in Business, Politics, and Everyday Life*. His second book, *Co-opetition*, written with Adam Brandenburger, is an extension of the article included in this collection. Professor Nalebuff applies game theory in his teaching, research, consulting work with businesses on strategy, and antitrust litigation.

C. K. PRAHALAD is the Harvey C. Fruehauf Professor of Business Administration at the University of Michigan Business School. His research focuses on the role and value-added of top management in large diversified, multinational corporations. He has also consulted with numerous firms worldwide. Professor Prahalad is the coauthor, with Gary Hamel, of *Competing for the Future*, which was named the Best-selling Business Book of the Year in 1994 by *Business Week* and has been translated into fourteen languages. He is also the author of many award-winning articles, such as "Strategic Intent" and "The Core Competence of the Corporation," which won McKinsey Prizes in 1989 and 1990, respectively.

PATRICK VIGUERIE is a principal in the Atlanta office of McKinsey & Company, where he serves clients in a wide range of industries, including telecommunications, electronics, and chemicals. As one of the leaders of McKinsey's strategy practice, he has led the firm's thinking in the area of strategy under uncertainty. Mr. Viguerie is also the leader of McKinsey's microeconomics practice, which brings leading-edge analytical capabilities such as game theory to client applications.

# Index